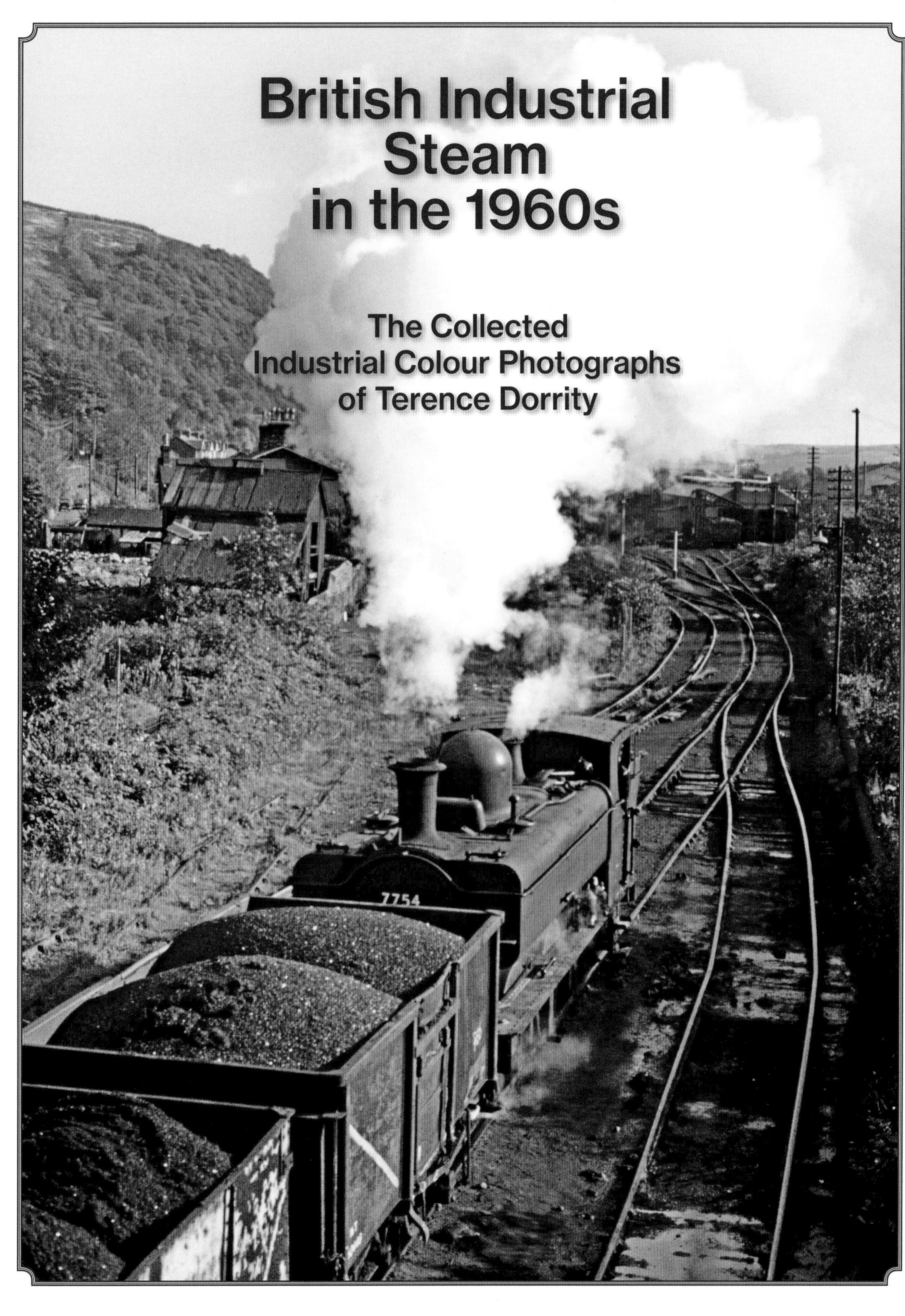

British Industrial Steam in the 1960s

The Collected Industrial Colour Photographs of Terence Dorrity

Lightmoor Press

British Industrial Steam in the 1960s

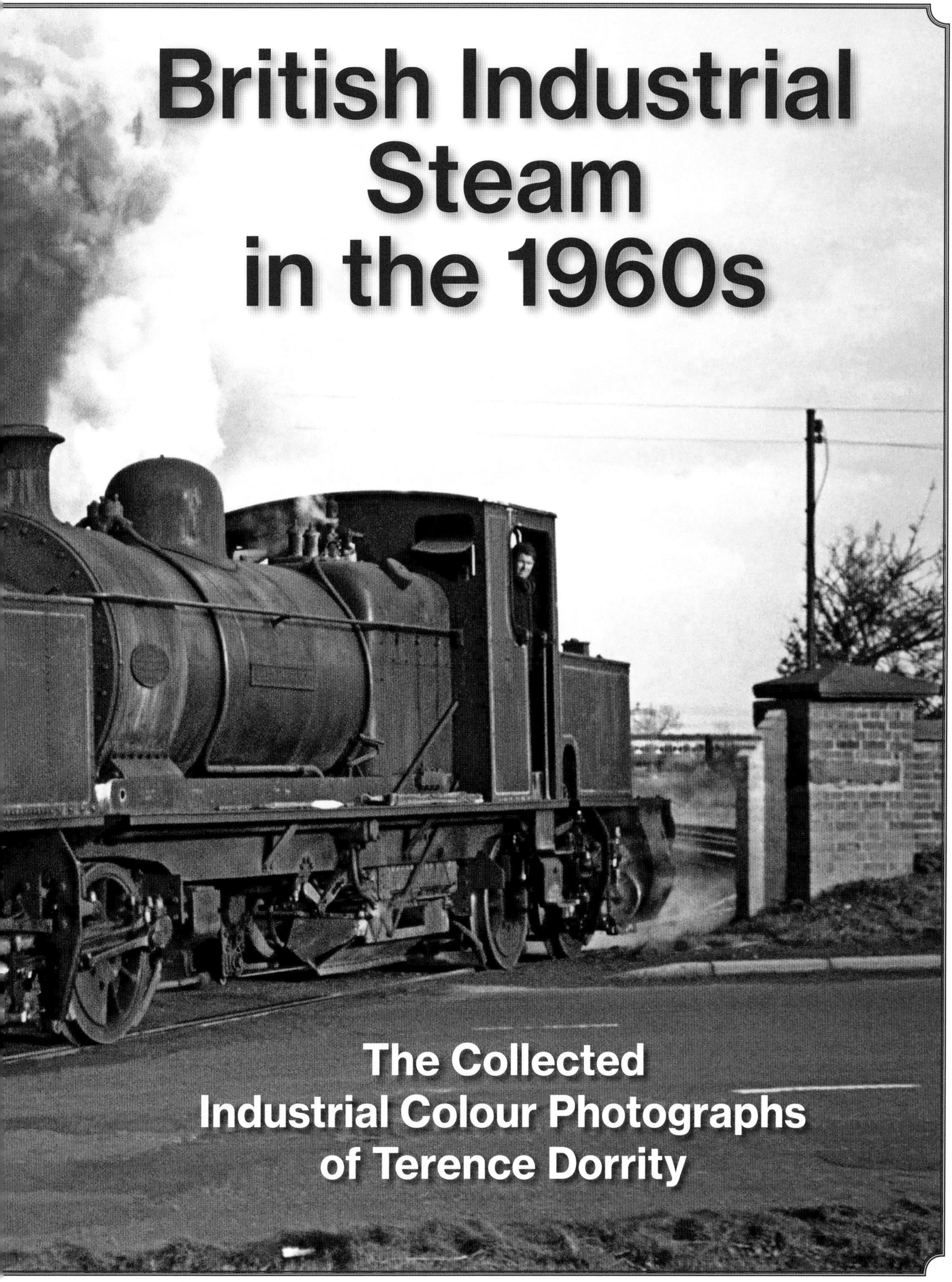

The Collected Industrial Colour Photographs of Terence Dorrity

Contents

Introduction 7
References 10

Part One: England

1 **The Oxfordshire Ironstone Company 11**

2 **Ironstone Quarries and Steelworks 25**
Stewarts & Lloyds Corby Iron & Steel Works • Stewarts & Lloyds Minerals Ltd, Corby Quarries • Pitsford Ironstone Quarries • Staveley Minerals Ltd, Cranford Quarries • Staveley Minerals Ltd, Loddington Quarries • Park Gate Iron & Steel Co. Ltd, Charwelton Ironstone Quarries • Byfield Ironstone Co. Ltd, Byfield Quarries • South Durham Steel & Iron Co. Ltd, Irchester Ironstone Quarries • Stewarts & Lloyds Springvale Furnaces at Bilston • Stewarts & Lloyds Bromford Bridge Tube Works, Erdington • Hodbarrow Haematite Mine and Millom Ironworks •

3 **National Coal Board. The Warwickshire Coalfield 43**
Baddesley Colliery, Baxterley • Birch Coppice Colliery, Dordon • Arley Colliery • Coventry Colliery, Keresley • Coventry Homefire Plant • Haunchwood Colliery, Nuneaton • Newdigate Colliery, Bedworth • Pooley Hall Colliery, Polesworth •

4 **National Coal Board. The Cannock Chase Coalfield 65**
Cannock Chase Central Workshops • Grove Colliery, Wyrley • Littleton Colliery, Huntington • Cannock Chase Railway Rawnsley Shed and Cannock Wood Colliery • Walsall Wood Colliery • West Cannock No. 5 Colliery, Hednesford •

5 **National Coal Board North and South 75**
Ravensworth Ann Colliery near Gateshead • Wearmouth Colliery • Seaham Colliery • Seaham Harbour Dock Co. Ltd • Kilmersdon Colliery in Somerset •

6 **Midlands Power Production - Electricity and Gas 87**
Central Electricity Generating Board, Leicester Electricity Generating Station • Central Electricity Generating Board, Nechells Generating Station, Birmingham • Central Electricity Generating Board, Hams Hall Power Station, Warwickshire • West Midlands Gas Board, Windsor Street Gas Works, Birmingham • West Midlands Gas Board, Nechells East (Saltley) Gas Works • West Midlands Gas Board, Nechells (West) Gas Works • West Midlands Gas Board, Soho Gas Works, Smethwick • West Midlands Gas Board, Wolverhampton Gas Works •

7 **West Midlands Industry. Cars, Tyres, Paper, Cement and Chocolate 99**
The British Motor Corporation Austin Motor Works in Longbridge • Dunlop Rubber Company Ltd, Fort Dunlop • Cadbury Brothers, Bournville • Alders (Tamworth) Ltd Paper Mill • Rugby Portland Cement Works, New Bilton • Associated Portland Cement Manufacturers Ltd, Harbury Cement Works •

8 **The South of England 111**
Beckton Gas Works and Beckton Products Works • United Glass Ltd, Charlton Works • Central Electricity Generating Board, Bow Power Station • Shipton-on-Cherwell Cement Works and Quarry • Associated Portland Cement Manufacturers Holborough Works, Snodland • Howard Farrow Ltd, Colindale Plant Depot, Hendon • Bowaters Pulp & Paper Mills, Sittingbourne • James Hodson & Sons Flour Mill, Robertsbridge • Corralls Coal Merchants, Southampton • Cheltenham Gloucester Road Gas Works • In the Scrapyard • Industrial Preservation •

9 **Industrial Narrow Gauge Miscellany 129**
Wellingborough Ironstone Quarries • Kettering Ironstone Quarries • Bowater's Railway • The First Garratt •

Part Two: Scotland

10 **The National Coal Board Waterside System in Ayrshire 145**

11 **National Coal Board Scottish Collieries 153**
Knockshinnoch Castle and Bank Collieries, Ayrshire • The Arniston Withdrawn Machinery Store at Gorebridge, Midlothian • Newbattle Central Workshops and Lady Victoria Colliery, Newtongrange, Midlothian • Kinneil Colliery, Bo'ness, West Lothian • Cowdenbeath Central Workshops, Fife •

12 **Iron and Steel, Power Production and a Distillery** 163
Bairds & Scottish Steel Northburn Works and Gartsherrie Works, Coatbridge, Lanarkshire • The South of Scotland Electricity Board, Yoker Power Station, Glasgow • Scottish Gas Board, Provan Gas Works, Glasgow • Scottish Gas Board, Sandilands Gas Works, Aberdeen • Scottish Malt Distillers Balmenach Distillery, Morayshire •

Part Three: Wales

13 **National Coal Board Collieries in Gwent** 181
Hafodrynys Colliery • Blaenavon Colliery • Celynen North Colliery • Blaenserchan Colliery and the Talywain Railway •

14 **National Coal Board Collieries in Glamorgan** 191
Bargoed Colliery • Deep Navigation Colliery • Mardy Colliery • Aberaman Works • Merthyr Vale Colliery • Mountain Ash Railways •

15 **Welsh Industry** 209
Fairfield Engineering & Shipbuilding, Chepstow, Monmouthshire • Bird's Scrapyard at Pontymister, Gwent • Richard Thomas & Baldwins Ltd, Pontardawe Tinplate Works, West Glamorgan • British Steel Corporation, Abercarn Works, Gwent • Guest, Keen & Nettlefolds Brymbo Steelworks, Denbighshire •

16 **Narrow Gauge. The North Wales Slate Quarries** 215
Dorothea Slate Quarries, Nantlle • Dinorwic Quarries, Llanberis • Penrhyn Quarries, Bethesda •

Scottish Malt Distillers' Andrew Barclay Works No. 2020 heads light towards Balmenach Distillery along the branch from Cromdale. *Sunday 27th August 1965*

HALF TITLE PAGE: Ex-Great Western Railway 0-6-0 pannier tank No. 7754 was hard at work at Mountain Ash Deep Duffryn Colliery. It was built for the GWR by the North British Locomotive Company in 1930 (Works No. 24042) and was withdrawn by British Railways in 1959 and sold to the NCB for use at Windsor Colliery. After moves to Llanbradach, Ogilvie, Elliot and Talywain, it had been transferred to Mountain Ash five months before this photograph was taken. *Wednesday 21st October 1970*

TITLE SPREAD: The distinctive 0-4-4-0 Beyer Garratt *William Francis* crossing the A5 'Watling Street' heading for the Baddesley Colliery exchange sidings to collect some wagons. There were no gates or signals at the level crossing over this busy main road so the fast moving traffic was brought to a halt by waving a red flag! A train can be seen passing by on the West Coast Main Line in the background. *Thursday 2nd January 1964*

Published by
LIGHTMOOR PRESS

British Library Cataloguing-in-Publication Data.
A catalogue record for this book is available from the British Library
ISBN: 97819038 94 8
Designed by Ade Haines and Jess Taylor.

LIGHTMOOR PRESS
Unit 144B, Harbour Road Trading Estate, Lydney, Gloucestershire GL15 4EJ
www.lightmoor.co.uk / info@lightmoor.co.uk
Lightmoor Press is an imprint of Black Dwarf Lightmoor Publications Ltd
Printed in Poland
www.lfbookservices.co.uk

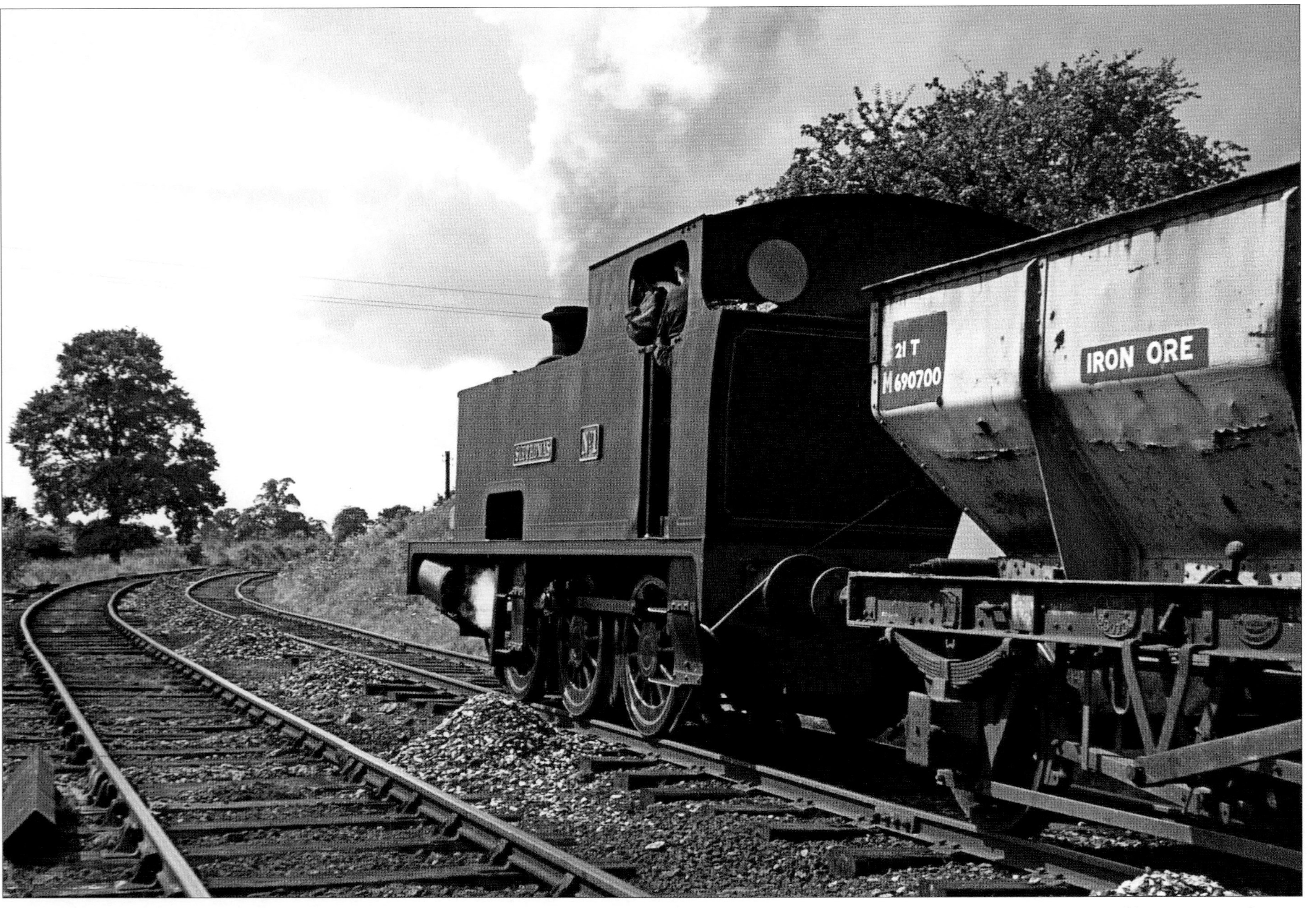

Oxfordshire Ironstone Company Ltd No. 1 ***Sir Thomas*** was hard at work near Pinhill Farm hauling a train of empties from the exchange sidings on the ex-Great Western Railway Paddington to Birmingham Snow Hill main line, just north of Banbury, to the quarry crusher at Wroxton. *Thursday 15th August 1963*

Introduction

The analogy of industrial railway systems as small twigs connected to the branches and trunk routes of, what was in the 1960s, British Railways is very tempting, though perhaps extending this metaphor to green leaves to describe steelworks, collieries and gas works would be a step too far! These 'twigs' were much less glamorous than their main-line counterparts but they were the essential final link in the system as they were the destination of the heavy goods trains that were often delivering massive quantities of raw materials such as coal and iron ore from their source to the plants and factories that depended on them. They were also the starting point of the distribution of finished products such as cars. In addition, there were often internal railway systems enabling movement within the sites.

I lived in the famously non-industrial tourist town of Stratford-upon-Avon where 'Castles' on the Wolverhampton Low Level to Penzance 'Cornishman' were the main attraction for the local railway enthusiasts. However, broadening my interest to include industrial railways I soon discovered that there were Bagnalls, Pecketts, Barclays and much more within very easy reach of the town. The industrial conurbation around Birmingham and the Black Country as well as the collieries in the National Coal Board Warwickshire Area to the north of the county were easily accessible on a day out. There was also a major industrial system in the countryside just eighteen miles away. I had not known of its existence until one day in the late 1950s when I was on the way to Banbury as a passenger in a car and I was surprised to see plumes of steam coming from the fields near Wroxton. This turned out to be from locomotives on the Oxfordshire Ironstone Quarries system which had a considerable fleet that worked in the quarries and hauled trains of iron ore along the system's main line to the British Railways exchange sidings. All of these are well represented in this book.

At this point I would like to thank my late father who made

The W.G. Bagnall modified Meyer articulated 0-4-4-0 side tank *Monarch* at work at Bowater's Ridham Dock. *Monday 30th December 1963*

R.&W. Hawthorn, Leslie & Co. Ltd 0-6-0 side tank *Jean* on duty at Wearmouth Colliery, Sunderland. *Monday 18th July 1966*

it possible for me to visit some industrial sites before I was old enough to do so on my own or with friends. He was not in the least interested in the, more often than not, filthy objects of my enthusiasm but he indulged it on several occasions when he persuaded gatemen to let us pass and then waited patiently in the rain, industrial odours and grime of gas works and factories no doubt wishing he was somewhere else. One site of special interest for which he arranged three visits over a number of years through a business contact was the impressive Stewarts and Lloyds Springvale steelworks at Bilston with its fleet of Andrew Barclay half-cab saddle tanks where a huge new furnace called 'Elisabeth' had been inaugurated in 1954.

I was already reasonably well informed because I had obtained a copy of the Birmingham Locomotive Club Pocket Book A *Industrial Locomotives of the West Midlands* which enabled me to seek out many locomotives in service in the area. Copies of the Pocket Book series covering other areas quickly expanded my geographical reach as I took advantage of visits to see friends and relatives to 'add on' an industrial site. More targeted visits were arranged either with a friend's or, later, my own transport as part of a more general railway trip or on specific visits to industrial sites further away from home down to the Southern Counties, west to North and South Wales and as far north as Aberdeen and the Balmenach Distillery near Granton-on-Spey in Morayshire.

Just as was the case with the main line 'Big Four' railway companies that had been nationalised as British Railways in 1948, many industrial railways were state owned when the photographs in this book were taken. 'Boards' had been established to manage the utility suppliers taken into public ownership after the Second World War. Important among these were the providers of the power that was essential to keep the wheels of industry turning as well as for domestic use. In the pre natural, or North Sea, gas era the Regional Gas Boards produced coal, otherwise known as town, gas. The Central Electricity Generating Board (successor to the Central Electricity Authority, formerly the British Electricity Authority) in England and Wales and the South of Scotland Electricity Board provided most electricity from coal-fired power stations even though there was some nuclear power generation and the North of Scotland Hydro-Electric Board lived up to its name. Most of these plants needed locomotives to receive the coal from which the power was produced and which was delivered from collieries to the power station and gas works exchange sidings by British Railways. The largest employer of steam locomotives by far was the National Coal Board which had been created on 'Vesting Day', 1st January 1947. Since the collieries provided coal to other industries, it is not a surprise that they almost exclusively used coal-fired steam engines after most other industrial railways had either turned to diesel power or been closed. A major industry, steel, had been subject to post-war nationalisation in 1951 but most had been sold back to private companies. However, the steel industry was re-nationalised as the British Steel Corporation in 1967 which led to rationalisation and closures not only of works but also the associated iron ore quarries which were already suffering from the competition of higher grade imported ore. There were, of course, many private industries with internal rail systems and photographs in this book were taken at cement works, iron ore and slate quarries, tinplate works, paper mills, a flour mill, a glass works, docks and even a distillery as well as a number of factories belonging to household names such as Cadbury at Bournville, the British Motor Corporation Austin works at Longbridge and Dunlop.

There was a remarkable lack of standardisation even within the 'boards'. This was because most of the locomotives had originated with the pre-nationalisation companies and had been obtained from different builders. Some, the Peckett 'W3', 'W4' and 'OX' Types for example, were 'off the peg' designs whereas others, like the large ex-Steel Company of Wales W.G. Bagnall built locomotives seen at Austin's Longbridge plant, were apparently designed to suit a specific need. Most were saddle tanks but there were side tanks, well tanks and even ex-Great Western Railway pannier tanks. The nearest to a 'Standard' design was the Robert Riddles wartime development of the Hunslet '50550' Type 0-6-0 saddle tank which originally entered service as a War Department locomotive built, despite the name, by several manufacturers. Many of these Hunslet 'Austerities' were sold off to industrial railways when no longer required after the war and yet more of this successful design were constructed until as late as 1964. Some railway enthusiasts refer to them as the 'J94' Class because seventy-five of the type were purchased from the War Department by the London and North Eastern Railway in 1946 and given that label but the ones in industrial service, with the exception of six sold on to the NCB by the LNER, were not. Some of these were among the last steam locomotives in use but despite their attraction I am pleased I was fortunate enough to see and photograph a wide variety of types built by many manufactures, the results of which you will find in this book.

The earliest photographs in this book were taken with the Kodak Retinette, 35mm camera with Schneider-Kreuznach Reomar 1:3.5 45mm lens (centre), followed by the Taron Marquise 35mm camera with Taromar 1:1.8 45mm lens (right) and lastly with the Mamiya Prismat CPH 35mm SLR camera with Mamiya Sekor 1:1.9 48mm lens (left).

Along with the products of the major locomotive builders, – Peckett, Hunslet, Bagnall and Barclay among others – there were also rarer examples from some smaller constructors such as Gibb and Hogg of Airdrie; Lilleshall Co. Ltd of Oakengates; Edward Borrows and Sons, Providence Works, Sutton near St. Helens; Stephen Lewin of Poole; Fox, Walker of Bristol; Grant, Richie & Co. of Kilmarnock; and Aveling and Porter of Rochester. Among the interesting finds were some nineteenth century veterans still going strong and unusual locomotives including *William Francis*, the Beyer Peacock 0-4-4-0 Beyer Garratt at Baddesley Colliery, 'ogee' tank locomotives and survivors bought second hand from the main line railway companies. Add to these the last remaining narrow gauge industrial systems, street running in Aberdeen and extensive workings such as the National Coal Board Waterside system and the Oxfordshire Ironstone Railway and there really was still a lot of interesting motive power variety to be seen in the 1960s. Most of this would be gone or just hanging on for a few more years, usually in a dilapidated state, as the decade ended.

I took some black and white photographs with my trusty Kodak Brownie Cresta 120 roll film camera before I graduated to 35mm when I obtained a Kodak Retinette. Very limited amounts of colour slide film followed in 1960 when the rather slow 12 ASA Kodachrome was the most popular brand. This was replaced by Kodachrome II and Kodachrome X with, each time, an increase in ASA speed. Industrial locomotives do not, of course, move at high speed but this made photography in poorer light conditions more successful. I mainly relied on Kodachrome and Agfa CT18 film although I tried other makes in small quantities: Ilford, Perutz and High Speed Ektachrome. Earlier photos taken on Agfa film have lasted the more than fifty years reasonably well but some of the later ones have very annoyingly suffered badly from colour deterioration and can be grainy so have not been considered suitable for this book.

Peckett 0-4-0 saddle tank No. 67 *NCB Pelaw*, catches the early morning sun at Ravensworth Ann Colliery in Co. Durham. *Monday 18th July 1966*

References

I am fortunate that I scrupulously kept detailed 'where, when and what' notes at the time I photographed the locomotives although I could not possibly have foreseen how useful these would be fifty or sixty years later on. It is even more fortunate that I still have them! I took the notes with the aid of the little Birmingham Locomotive Club pocket books which were a very practical aid in finding and identifying sites and their locomotives. More recently, the excellent Industrial Locomotive Society handbooks listed below were an invaluable resource in researching and updating details of the origins and disposals of locomotives. Additional information about those that have since been preserved comes from the web pages of the societies concerned and which are mentioned in the captions in this book.

Birmingham Locomotive Club Pocket Books:
6: *Industrial Locomotives of South Wales*, 1951
A: *Industrial Locomotives of the West Midlands*, 1957
B: *Industrial Locomotives of Southern England*, 1958
C: *Industrial Locomotives of South-Eastern England*, 1958
D: *Industrial Locomotives of Eastern England*, 1960

Industrial Railway Society Handbooks:
L: *Industrial Locomotives of Durham*, compiled by Colin E. Mountford and L.G. Charlton, 1977
N: *Industrial Locomotives of Scotland*, edited by Alan Bridges, 1976
WM: *Industrial Locomotives of West Midlands*, compiled by R.A. Shill, 1992
Industrial Locomotives of North Wales, compiled by V.J. Bradley, 1992
Industrial Locomotives of South Staffordshire, compiled by R.A. Shill, 1993
Industrial Locomotives of West Glamorgan, compiled by Martin Potts & G.W. Green, 1996
Industrial Locomotives of Gwent, compiled by Geoffrey Hill & Gordon Green, 1999
Industrial Locomotives of Mid and South Glamorgan, compiled by Geoffrey Hill, 2007
Industrial Locomotives of Buckinghamshire, Bedfordshire and Northamptonshire, compiled by Robin Waywell, 2001
Industrial Railways and Locomotives of Hertfordshire & Middlesex, compiled by Robin Waywell, 2007
Industrial Railways and Locomotives of the County of London, compiled by Robin Waywell & Frank Jux, 2008
Industrial Railways and Locomotives of Kent, Robin Waywell, 2016
Industrial Railways and Locomotives of Warwickshire, Industrial Railway Society preliminary draft, 2003

Other Books Consulted:
The Ironstone Quarries of the Midlands, Eric Tonks, Runpast, 1988
Part I. History, Operation and Railways
Part II. The Oxfordshire Field
Jowett's Railway Atlas, Alan Jowett, Guild Publishing, 1989
Ordnance Survey One Inch Maps. Mostly seventh series.

Useful Websites:
http://chasewaterstuff.wordpress.com
http://www.warwickshirerailways.com
http://www.nuneatonhistory.com/brickyards-quarries--collieries-extractive-industries.html
https://en.wikipedia.org/wiki/List_of_Peckett_and_Sons_railway_locomotives
preservedbritishsteamlocomotives.com/industrial-locomotives/
https://www.rocks-by-rail.org/

Ex-British Railways 0-6-0 pannier tank No. 1501 in National Coal Board service at Coventry (Keresley) Colliery. ***Monday 9th August 1965***

Part One: England

Chapter 1

The Oxfordshire Ironstone Company

The Oxfordshire Ironstone Company quarry system was one of the largest in the country, second only to Corby, and it was served by a 'real' railway. The nearly four mile long double track main line with its heavy trains, guards van at the rear, hauled by powerful locomotives along with another, separate, fleet of smaller engines serving the quarries made for a very interesting range of stock and operation. Most of the locomotives were saddle tanks but two, out of originally three, 0-6-0 side tanks and a little-used 4-wheeled vertical boiler Sentinel added variety. The 0-6-0 main line locomotives, mostly carrying boys' names, were stabled at a locomotive shed at Pinhill (or Penhill) and the 0-4-0 quarry locomotives, in the main carrying girls' names, were shedded at Wroxton where the headquarters of the quarry company was situated.

The Oxfordshire Ironstone Railway main line ran from the exchange sidings on the ex-Great Western Railway Paddington to Birmingham Snow Hill main line, just north of Banbury, to the quarry crusher at Wroxton and was equipped as a fully-fledged railway with signals, gradient posts, bridges and level crossings. Doubling of the full length was completed in 1953. Unusually in Britain, though not unknown on industrial systems, the trains ran on the right hand side and made a fine sight for anyone travelling along the A422 Stratford-upon-Avon to Banbury road near Wroxton. Branches went into the quarries at Alkerton, Balscott (also known as Balscote), and Hornton.

The workings extracting Marlstone, also called Hornton or Banbury Ironstone, from the middle lias geological strata were started during the First World War and the system was closed fifty years later, in September 1967. This closure came as a surprise to many as eleven brand new diesel locomotives, to add to two bought earlier for trials, had arrived in 1964 and 1965 to replace the steam fleet. The OIC was not alone in this demise. Many of the iron ore quarries in Northamptonshire also closed around this time as they became redundant when demand fell as more and more cheaper and higher quality ore was imported and also as the inevitable consequence of the rationalisation of the steel industry following the creation of the nationalised British Steel Corporation on 28th July 1967.

Pride of the line, the now preserved Oxfordshire Ironstone Company Ltd No. 1 *Sir Thomas*, a 16 x 24in. outside cylinder 0-6-0 side tank locomotive, was built by Hudswell, Clarke & Co. of Leeds in 1918 with the Works No. 1334. On a fine summer day it was hard at work near Pinhill Farm hauling a train of empties from the exchange sidings to the quarry crusher at Wroxton. *Sir Thomas* was one of two similar locomotives originally ordered by the Inland Waterways and Docks Executive during the First World War. As they were no longer required at the end of the war, in 1918, they became the first OIC owned locomotives on the system. The other one, No. 2 *Lord North*, was scrapped in 1958. *Thursday 15th August 1963*

The weather on the Oxfordshire Ironstone Railway was not always as good as in August! Four months later, on a bitterly cold Christmas Eve, No. 1 ***Sir Thomas*** was near the water tank at Pinhill Farm, sometimes referred to as Penhill Farm. Note the brazier by the water column, presumably an attempt to keep it from freezing up. ***Sir Thomas*** was named after Sir Thomas Pope who was the first owner of Wroxton Abbey which was near the central facilities of the railway. *Tuesday 24th December 1963*

Fortunately, ***Sir Thomas*** has been preserved and has resided at the Buckingham Railway Centre since June 1969 where it was used on some of the first trains at the Quainton Road site. It is seen here pulling an open truck and guards van full of enthusiasts at the Quainton Road Society's first steam (long) weekend, on Bank Holiday Monday. *Monday 1st September 1969*

Like ***Sir Thomas*** and ***Lord North,*** No. 3 ***The President*** was a 16 x 24in. outside cylinder 0-6-0 side tank locomotive built by Hudswell, Clarke & Co. It was supplied new to Oxfordshire Ironstone in 1923, with the Works No. 1419. It was passing the Alcan aluminium works by the Southam Road near Banbury returning to Wroxton with a train of empties. It was scrapped on site by James Friswell of Banbury in the autumn of 1965. *Monday 26th April 1965*

Another Oxfordshire Ironstone '*Sir*' was the 16 x 24in. outside cylinder Peckett 0-6-0 saddle tank ***Sir Charles*** which was built in 1938 with the Works No. 1943. Named after Sir Charles Wright, a chairman of the OIC, it is seen here on the main line at Horley hauling a loaded train bound for the exchange sidings. ***Sir Charles*** was delivered new to Oxfordshire Ironstone and, like ***The President***, was scrapped on site by James Friswell of Banbury in the autumn of 1965. *Tuesday 13th April 1965*

On Christmas Eve, ***Sir Charles*** was shunting brake van No. 5 at Wroxton. The crew had obviously taken emergency measures to keep the cab warm! The van was ex-Great Western Railway No. 68619 built at Swindon in 1924, one of a number acquired when vacuum braking was introduced around this time to allow longer trains on the line. In fact ***Sir Charles*** had been vacuum fitted only a few weeks earlier. I was lucky enough to be presented with a nameplate from this locomotive after it was withdrawn thanks to Eric Tonks of the Birmingham Locomotive Club. *Tuesday 24th December 1963*

John was also in steam with a boarded-up cab at Wroxton that cold Christmas Eve in 1963. It was a 14 x 22in. outside cylinder 0-6-0 saddle tank locomotive built by Peckett in 1941 with the Works No. 1981. *John* had been supplied new to OIC and was originally named *Joan* but this was changed to *John* in 1957 when it was decided to give the girls' names to the 0-4-0s and the boys' names to the 0-6-0s. It was sent to G. Cohen, Cransley, for scrap in September 1965.
Tuesday 24th December 1963

Allan, right, a Peckett 16 x 24in. outside cylinder 0-6-0 saddle tank built 1941 with the Works No. 1997, hauling a train of empty wagons meets its younger brother, *Frank*, a 16 x 22in. inside cylinder Hunslet Engine Co. 0-6-0 saddle tank of 1958 with the Works No. 3872, in charge of a loaded train on the main line at Pinhill Farm. Locomotives ran bunker first with loaded trains towards the exchange sidings and boiler first on the return with the empties.
Tuesday 24th December 1963

Seen again at Horley sixteen months later, Oxfordshire Ironstone 0-6-0 saddle tank ***Frank*** headed a loaded morning train bound for the exchange sidings. ***Frank*** was the last steam locomotive to be delivered new to Oxfordshire Ironstone, in November 1958. It was scrapped on site when less than seven years old by James Friswell of Banbury in the autumn of 1965. *Monday 26th April 1965*

Frank was seen a little later, this time from the Southam Road bridge, clearly showing the unusual running on the right-hand side of the double track line. *Monday 26th April 1965*

Allan was also in action again hauling loaded wagons at Horley. It still showed some damage sustained in an accident when it was derailed and ended up on its side. Fortunately nobody was seriously injured. *Monday 26th April 1965*

No. 5 *Basic*, a Peckett 16 x 24in. outside cylinder 0-6-0 saddle tank built in 1935 with the Works No. 1867, runs round at the interchange sidings. Prior to April 1963 locomotives had not run round but propelled the empty wagons back uphill to Wroxton. The acquisition of the ex-Great Western Railway brake vans made a runaway unlikely so the locomotives could haul the trains up the incline. ***Basic*** had been delivered new to Oxfordshire Ironstone and it was scrapped on site by James Friswell of Banbury in the autumn of 1965. *Thursday 15th August 1963*

No. 2 *Joan* was an Avonside Engine Co. 'SS3' Type 14 x 20in. outside cylinder 0-4-0 saddle tank of 1919 with the Works No. 1822. It is seen here on a train of dumpcar trucks at Wroxton on Christmas Eve. This locomotive was supplied new to the Margam Iron and Steel Works, Port Talbot, then owned by British (Guest, Keen, Baldwins) Iron & Steel Co. Ltd, as their No. 2. It moved on to Oxfordshire Ironstone from Margam Works, which was by then owned by the Steel Company of Wales, in January 1957 with the number 303, which as can be seen was also still being carried on the rear of the cab. It was sent for scrap to G. Cohen, Cransley, in September 1965. *Tuesday 24th December 1963*

On that same bitterly cold Christmas Eve in 1963, *Grace*, a 14 x 22in. outside cylinder 0-4-0 saddle tank built by Peckett in 1936 with the Works No. 1894, was working on trains of dumpcars for internal use from the quarries to the crusher at Wroxton. Originally supplied new to OIC, it was sent, like *Joan*, to G. Cohen, Cransley, for scrap in September 1965. *Tuesday 24th December 1963*

No. 4 ***The Dean*** was an older Hunslet Engine Co. 16 x 22in. inside cylinder 0-6-0 saddle tank locomotive built in 1926 with the Works No. 1496. It was resting at Pinhill Farm on a very frosty Saturday. One of the last OIC locomotives to survive, it was scrapped on site by James Friswell of Banbury in the spring of 1969. The land quarried was leased from Trinity and Christchurch Colleges, Oxford, which explains the names of ***The Dean*** and ***The Bursar***. *Saturday 24th February 1962*

Newlay was Hunslet Engine Co. 15 x 20in. outside cylinder 0-4-0 saddle tank number 1292 built in 1917. It had come to the OIC system from the Steel Company of Wales at Margam in May 1951 although it had earlier worked at Pantmawr Quarry in Mid Glamorgan and the Newlay Wheel Co. Ltd of Leeds, where it got its name. It had clearly already been withdrawn from service with its coupling rods removed when seen at Wroxton. It was cut up there in April the following year by E.L. Pitt & Co. (Coventry) Ltd. *Christmas Eve 1963*

Betty, an 0-4-0 saddle tank with 14 x 22in. outside cylinders built in 1953 by Hudswell, Clarke, was working at Wroxton. It carried the Works No. 1869 and was delivered new to the OIC along with sister locomotive ***Barabel*** (Works No. 1868). It was sent to G. Cohen at Cransley for scrap in September 1965. *Thursday 15th August 1963*

Soon afterwards on that Thursday, ***Betty*** ran alongside the Wroxton buildings hauling a train of dumpcars used in the quarry areas. This was exactly one week after the Great Train Robbery so there were likely to have been plenty of obvious silly jokes about stopping the train! Wroxton was the headquarters of the quarry company and where the locomotive sheds for the 0-4-0 quarry locomotives and the main works were sited. There was a second shed at Pinhill where the 0-6-0 main line locomotives were stabled. *Thursday 15th August 1963*

Branches ran from the Oxfordshire Ironstone quarries at Alkerton, Balscott, and Hornton to the crusher at Wroxton. ***Maud*** is seen working along one of these branches. The relatively temporary nature of these lines is clear because, unlike the higher standard of the main line, the track is not laid on ballast. Note the buckeye coupling for use with the dumpcars. *Thursday 15th August 1963*

Maud was a 14 x 22in. outside cylinder Peckett 0-4-0 saddle tank built in 1938 with the Works No. 1937. It had been delivered new to the OIC and, along with *Barabel*, *Betty* and others, was sent to G. Cohen, Cransley, for scrap in September 1965. Note the locomotive roster on the Wroxton signal box showing *Maud* and *Betty* on duty on Wednesday, but it was Thursday. *Thursday 15th August 1963*

Looking very different to the other steam locomotives on the system, ***Phyllis*** was out of steam at Wroxton as it had been since the end of 1960 because it was not really powerful enough for its duties. This was a 200hp 4-wheel vertical boiler locomotive built by Sentinel (Shrewsbury) Ltd in 1956 with the Works No. 9615. It was sent with others to G. Cohen at Cransley for scrap in September 1965. *Sunday 22nd November 1964*

This sad line up at Wroxton with ***The Bursar*** at the head was truly the end of the line for steam which was replaced by thirteen 311hp 0-4-0 diesel-hydraulics, the first three from Sentinel and the rest from Rolls-Royce after it had taken over the Sentinel works. Eight of them had arrived by the time this photograph was taken. ***The Bursar,*** a Hunslet 14 x 20in. outside cylinder 0-6-0 saddle tank, had travelled far. Built in 1930 with the Works No. 1645, it had been used on the Haifa Harbour Works in Palestine (now Israel). It was rebuilt by Hunslet in 1940 and went to the OIC after the war, in November 1946. It was scrapped on site by James Friswell of Banbury in the spring of 1969. *Saturday 20th February 1965*

This was how the iron ore continued on its way to the steelworks. No. 6826 ***Nannerth Grange*** rounds the 'new' curve at Stratford-upon-Avon on a train of loaded iron ore tippler wagons heading for South Wales and passes No. 6834 ***Dummer Grange*** hauling a train of sheeted loaded wagons (coal?) east in the early afternoon. The opening of this curve in 1960 meant that iron ore trains to South Wales from quarries including Oxfordshire Ironstone near Banbury, plus other steel trains via Woodford Halse which had previously run along the by then closed section of the Stratford-upon-Avon & Midland Junction Railway line from Stratford to Broom Junction, could use the more direct Great Western Railway route via Honeybourne. Both of these 'Grange' Class locomotives were built by the GWR at Swindon Works in 1937. No. 6826 was withdrawn in May 1965 and No. 6834 in June 1964. *Wednesday 11th March 1964*

Chapter 2

Ironstone Quarries and Steelworks

Iron ore quarrying in the Oxfordshire and Northamptonshire area was quite extensive at the time and several iron and steel works had been established in Northamptonshire to take advantage of the abundance and proximity of the raw material to be found there. The sheer weight of the ore obviously lent itself to transport by rail and, inevitably, railway systems were constructed and provided with the fleets of locomotives needed both to work internally in the quarries and to deliver the ore. In a number of cases this was directly to the local iron works but in others it was from the quarries to exchange sidings with the main line where the onward journey was in the hands of British Railways.

The Stewarts & Lloyds Corby quarries system was even bigger than that of the Oxfordshire Ironstone Company. The ore was delivered directly to the Corby iron and steel works and this practice continued until 1980 when the huge blast furnaces went cold forever. There were several other interesting quarry railways in operation, including two which used narrow gauge steam engines at Kettering and Wellingborough. These latter can be seen in Chapter 9 which covers narrow gauge in England. All in all there was quite a variety of industrial steam locomotive types to be seen.

Looking smart in the yellow Corby steelworks livery, Stewarts & Lloyds No. 15, a 16 x 24in. outside cylinder 0-6-0 saddle tank built by Hawthorn, Leslie & Co. in 1934 with the Works No. 3836, in action. This locomotive was coal fired when delivered new to Corby but was later converted to oil burning. It was still in regular use in 1971 but it was scrapped in 1972, well after the works had become part of the nationalised British Steel Corporation in July 1968. This picture, taken from the Rockingham Road in Corby, also shows a main line BR diesel Sultzer Type 4 'Peak' at the head of a coal train in the passing loop on the ex-Midland Railway Manton to Kettering line next to the North Exchange Sidings. *Saturday 24th October 1964*

A fine panoramic view of the Corby steelworks. The nearest locomotive is No. 29, a 14 x 22in. outside cylinder 0-6-0 saddle tank built by Andrew Barclay of Kilmarnock in 1915 with the Works No. 1457. *Thursday 24th February 1966*

Stewarts & Lloyds Corby Iron & Steel Works

The vast Corby Iron and Steel Works was the destination for much of Northamptonshire's iron ore. It became part of the British Steel Corporation in July 1968. The first blast furnaces came into operation in 1910 but the works was greatly expanded in the 1930s when Stewarts & Lloyds decided to move a lot of production from Scotland to Corby causing many families to move to the town as well. Evidence of this still exists in the form of a pipe band and other local Scottish references. The North Exchange Sidings were alongside the works on the ex-Midland Railway Manton to Kettering line. After the steam locomotives were withdrawn the rail system continued to be worked by a large fleet of diesels which included some from the Oxfordshire Ironstone Railway and a few British Railways Swindon built Class '14' 0-6-0 diesel hydraulics. The last Corby blast furnace was shut down in April 1980.

Nearer the camera, Stewarts & Lloyds No. 29 is seen hauling empty slag ladles at Corby Iron and Steel Works. The blast furnaces can be seen to the left. This locomotive had earlier worked at Shell-Mex & BP Ltd, Trafford Park, Manchester and had been bought by Stewarts & Lloyds from Geo. Cohen, Sons & Co. Ltd at the end of 1939. It was scrapped in May 1967. *Thursday 24th February 1966*

No. 22 was a Robert Stephenson & Hawthorns of Newcastle 16 x 24in. outside cylinder 0-6-0 saddle tank built in 1940 with the Works No. 6944. Supplied new to Stewarts & Lloyds, it was seen here at Corby hauling a train of tube wagons as well as oil tank wagons that carried fuel for the Tube Works furnaces. This was one of about ten steam locomotives to pass into British Steel Corporation ownership in 1968 and it was one of the very last of the steam fleet to be scrapped, in the autumn of 1972. Unlike a number of the Corby locomotives this one remained coal burning to the end. *Thursday 24th February 1966*

Stewarts & Lloyds No. 39 ***Rhos***, painted in the quarry system green livery, is a 15 x 22in. outside cylinder Hudswell, Clarke & Co. Ltd '26T' 0-6-0 saddle tank with the Works No. 1308. It is seen here at the Stewarts & Lloyds Corby Quarries impressive eight-road Gretton Brook locomotive shed. It was delivered new to Lloyds Ironstone Co. Ltd, Corby, in January 1918. It worked away from home, at Glendon East Quarries, from 1952 to 1957. In 1968 ***Rhos*** was sold for preservation in Norfolk and it was later to be found on the Nene Valley Railway. It is now at the Rutland Railway Museum Rocks by Rail at Cottesmore. *Saturday 24th October 1964*

Stewarts & Lloyds Minerals Ltd, Corby Quarries

Identifiable by their green livery rather than the yellow of the steelworks stud, the quarry locomotives were based at a large engine shed at Gretton Brook with a works at Pen Green. Quarrying at the extensive Corby Quarries ended in January 1980 although production had already greatly decreased as more imported ore was used at the steelworks.

On the same day, No. 35, another green liveried Stewarts & Lloyds 0-6-0 saddle tank, was also in steam at the Corby Quarries Gretton Brook locomotive shed. This 15 x 22in. inside cylinder Manning, Wardle product, with the Works No. 1317, was supplied new in 1895 to Birmingham Corporation for work on the construction of the Elan Valley reservoir near Rhayader in Radnorshire where it carried the name *Rhiwnant*. When no longer required it was sold to Thos W. Ward Ltd and then bought by Lloyds Ironstone Co. Ltd Corby in 1912 and so it later became part of the Stewarts & Lloyds Minerals fleet at Corby Quarries. It went to the Foxfield Light Railway for preservation in October 1969. It has also been at Peak Rail and it has been reported to be at South Coast Steam at Portland in Dorset for restoration. *Saturday 24th October 1964*

No. 35 hauled an interesting mixed bag of rolling stock on the tool van train near to Gretton Brook on that Saturday. This was in complete contrast to sixty years earlier, on 21st July 1904, when as ***Rhiwnant*** it had a moment of fame as a Royal Engine hauling the Royal Train on its return trip along the Elan Valley Railway from the Craig Goch dam site, where King Edward VII and Queen Alexandra officially opened the Elan Valley Reservoir, to Rhayader. According to the Powys Digital History Project website, the trackside was lined with soldiers. The King turned an ornate handwheel at the filter beds near Elan Village to send water on its way along the 73 miles of the aqueduct to Birmingham. *Saturday 24th October 1964*

No. 46 ***Cardigan***, a 16 x 22in. inside cylinder 0-6-0 saddle tank built by Kitson & Co. Ltd at the Airedale Foundry in Leeds in 1933 with the Works No. 5473, was working hard delivering iron ore to Corby Works. ***Cardigan*** was delivered new to Stewarts & Lloyds Ltd for work at the Corby Iron and Steel Works. In November 1949 it was transferred to the Corby Ironstone Quarries pool. It was one of seven similar locomotives at Corby built by Kitson to a design by Manning, Wardle. All were named after Welsh towns. Three of its sister locomotives have been preserved: No. 44 ***Conway*** by the Middleton Railway, No. 45 ***Colwyn*** at the Northampton & Lamport Railway and No. 47 ***Carnarvon*** at the South Devon Railway. The steam fleet became redundant by the end of the decade as work was then done by diesels, many of them second-hand British Rail Class '14's. ***Cardigan*** was scrapped on site by George Cohen, Sons & Co. of Cransley in November 1969. Iron ore production at Corby Quarries ended at the start of 1980. *Thursday 24th February 1966*

Pitsford Ironstone Quarries

Quarrying started at Pitsford in 1923. The Pitsford Ironstone Co. had been taken over by Byfield Ironstone Co. Ltd the month before this photograph was taken. Rail connection was via an approximately mile long branch to the ex-London & North Western Railway Northampton to Market Harborough line. Although working ended in August 1965 two steam locomotives, an Avonside and a Hudswell, Clarke, remained on site until July 1966.

The venerable No. 2 was a 12 x 18in. outside cylinder Manning, Wardle 'H' Type 0-4-0 saddle tank built in 1871 with the Works No. 345. It had clearly already been withdrawn from service for some time when seen at Pitsford Ironstone Quarries. It had come to Pitsford from the Park Gate Iron and Steel Co. Ltd Charwelton Ironstone Quarries, where it was called *Holmes*, in the mid-1930s. Before Charwelton, it had been working at the Park Gate Ironworks in Rotherham, Yorkshire. It was scrapped in January 1964. *Thursday 6th November 1962*

Staveley Minerals Ltd, Cranford Quarries

Cranford Quarries became part of the Stewarts & Lloyds empire early in 1966 but quarrying ended quite soon afterwards, in August 1969. The rail connection was with the ex-Midland Railway line from Kettering to Cambridge.

Cranford No. 2 was, and fortunately still is, a 15 x 22in. outside cylinder 0-6-0 saddle tank built by W.G. Bagnall Ltd in 1942 with the Works No. 2668. It was originally ordered for the Ministry of Supply wartime Home Ore Scheme and was delivered new to the Cranford Ironstone Co. Ltd at Cranford Quarries in Northamptonshire in May the year it was built. It went into preservation when the quarries closed in August 1969; first near Northampton, then at Radstock and Carnforth. It was later based at the Embsay & Bolton Abbey Steam Railway and it also visited the North Yorkshire Moors Railway. Since October 2006 it is to be found at the Rutland Railway Museum Rocks by Rail at Cottesmore. *Thursday 6th November 1962*

No. 24 was also at the Staveley Minerals Ltd Cranford Quarries that day. This 15 x 22in. outside cylinder 0-6-0 saddle tank was built by Hudswell, Clarke & Co. Ltd of Leeds in 1926 with the Works No. 1579. It left the works in January 1927 and was delivered to the Frodingham Iron & Steel Co. Ltd at Scunthorpe in Lincolnshire. The locomotive had come to Cranford in November 1957 from what had by then become the Appleby Frodingham Steel Co. Ltd. It was scrapped in May 1968.
Thursday 6th November 1962

Staveley Minerals Ltd, Loddington Quarries

Quarrying near Loddington began at the end of the nineteenth century and continued until the quarries closed in 1963. The railway and equipment were mothballed for possible, but unrealised, future use. The track was removed in 1971.

Loddington No. 2, a 1942 built W. G. Bagnall 15 x 22in. outside cylinder 0-6-0 saddle tank with the Works No. 2655, was in action at Loddington Quarries. It was supplied new to the Byfield Ironstone Co. Ltd and originally named *Byfield No. 2*. Like *Cranford No. 2*, it was one of seven locomotives ordered by the Ministry of Supply for the Home Ore Scheme. It went to the Oxfordshire Ironstone Company in 1944 and then to the Loddington Quarries in January 1947 where it was renamed *Loddington No. 2* in 1956. When these quarries closed in 1963 it was transferred to Cranfield Quarries and when these closed in turn, in 1969, it was sold to Hunt & Co. of Hinckley and renamed *Huntsman*. It later went to the Gloucestershire and Warwickshire Railway where it became *Byfield No. 2* once again. In September 2002 it moved on to the Plym Valley Railway. *Thursday 6th November 1962*

Park Gate Iron & Steel Co. Ltd, Charwelton Ironstone Quarries

The quarry line ran to a yard at Charwelton station on the ex-Great Central Railway main line between Rugby and Aylesbury. The Charwelton railway system had closed on 18th November 1961. This was intended to be a temporary situation as demand for the ore was low at the time but in June 1963 track lifting began, definitively rendering the locomotives redundant and both were scrapped on site at the end of 1963.

No. 8 was an attractive 14 x 20in. outside cylinder 0-4-0 saddle tank built by the Yorkshire Engine Co. in 1905 with the Works No. 784. Photographed here just a few weeks before it was scrapped on site at the Park Gate Iron & Steel Co. Ltd Charwelton Ironstone Quarries in Northamptonshire, to where it had come from the Park Gate Ironworks, Rotherham, Yorkshire, in February 1952. *Saturday 14th September 1963*

No. 5 was positioned behind No. 8 at the Park Gate Iron & Steel Co. Ltd Charwelton Ironstone Quarries. This was a 12 x 18in. outside cylinder 0-4-0 saddle tank built by W.G. Bagnall in 1942 with the Works No. 2659. It had followed No. 8 from the Park Gate Ironworks, Rotherham, Yorkshire, in January 1957. It had a cut-down chimney and dome and a low cab. *Saturday 14th September 1963*

Byfield Ironstone Co. Ltd, Byfield Quarries

Byfield Quarry was connected by rail to the ex-Stratford-upon-Avon & Midland Junction Railway line from Fenny Compton to Towcester. The quarry closed in February 1965. One of the Byfield locomotives was the 1890 Manning, Wardle *Sir Berkeley* which now resides on the Keighley & Worth Valley Railway.

No. 3 ***Avonside*** was an Avonside Engine Co. 'B5' Type 14 ½ x 20in. outside cylinder 0-6-0 saddle tank built in 1924 with the Works No. 1919. It is seen here at Byfield Quarries in the autumn of 1963. No. 3 was delivered new to Staveley Ironworks, Derbyshire, but had been transferred to Byfield Quarries in the spring of 1960. The quarry closed in February 1965 and in the September the locomotive moved again, this time to Staveley Minerals Ltd at Cranford Ironstone Quarries where it was renamed ***Cranford***. That quarry closed in August 1969 and the locomotive was bought for preservation and went to the Foxfield Light Railway in January 1971. It later moved on to the Appleby Frodingham Railway Preservation Society at Scunthorpe steelworks.
Saturday 14th September 1963

Hiding in the bushes behind barbed wire and looking very sorry for itself at Byfield Quarries in 1963 was ***Byfield***, a 13 x 20in. inside cylinder 0-6-0 saddle tank built by Hudswell, Clarke in 1892 with the Works No. 347. It had come to Byfield from the Furness Shipbuilding Co. Ltd in County Durham a year or two after the First World War. At that time is was named ***Lance B Pain*** but it was renamed ***Byfield*** at the end of the 1920s and, apart from a few years, from 1951 to the end of 1956 when it worked at Charwelton Quarries, it remained at Byfield. Clearly already withdrawn from service long before this photograph was taken, it was scrapped in February 1965 at the same time as ore production at the quarry ceased.
Saturday 14th September 1963

South Durham Steel and Iron Co. Ltd, Irchester Ironstone Quarries

The Irchester Ironstone Quarries rail connection with the main line was at Wellingborough London Road station on the ex-London & North Western Railway Northampton to Peterborough line. The quarries closed in June 1969.

No. 7, an Andrew Barclay outside cylinder 0-4-0 saddle tank built in 1952 with the Works No. 2324, seen here working at the South Durham Steel & Iron Co. Ltd Irchester Ironstone Quarries. It had come to Irchester from the Cargo Fleet Ironworks at Middlesborough in July 1964. After it was withdrawn from service it was sent to Cohen's at Cransley where it was scrapped in September 1969, three months after the quarries had closed. Its sister locomotive No. 9, Works No. 2323 also built in 1952, has been preserved. *Thursday 24th February 1966*

Andrew Barclay 14 x 24in. outside cylinder 0-4-0 saddle tank locomotive *Clare* at Stewarts & Lloyds Springvale Furnaces. Its yellow livery was showing obvious signs of oil and the heat of the furnaces. Built in 1911 (Works No. 1235), *Clare* was delivered new to the Springvale furnaces when it was owned by Sir Alfred Hickman Ltd. It was scrapped at the end of 1963. Like the other Barclays at Springvale, *Clare* had a half-cab. *Sunday 30th September 1962*

Stewarts & Lloyds Ltd Springvale Furnaces at Bilston

There were two very large steelworks in the Black Country part of Staffordshire which became part of the West Midlands Metropolitan County in 1974 as a result of local government reorganisation. One was Round Oak at Brierley Hill, now the site of the extensive Merry Hill shopping centre. The other one was Stewarts & Lloyds Ltd Springvale Furnaces at Bilston which had been owned by Sir Alfred Hickman Ltd until 1921. The surviving steam fleet there in 1962 consisted of one Kerr, Stewart and seven Andrew Barclay 0-4-0 saddle tank locomotives which were ranged against twelve Yorkshire Engine Co. and two Ruston & Hornsby 0-4-0 diesel electric and two Ruston & Hornsby four-wheeled diesel mechanical shunters, one of which was out of use. The rail system was connected to the ex-Great Western Railway Dudley to Wolverhampton line. In 1954 a huge new blast furnace, replacing three smaller ones, had come into operation. Called Elisabeth after the daughter of the chairman of Stewarts

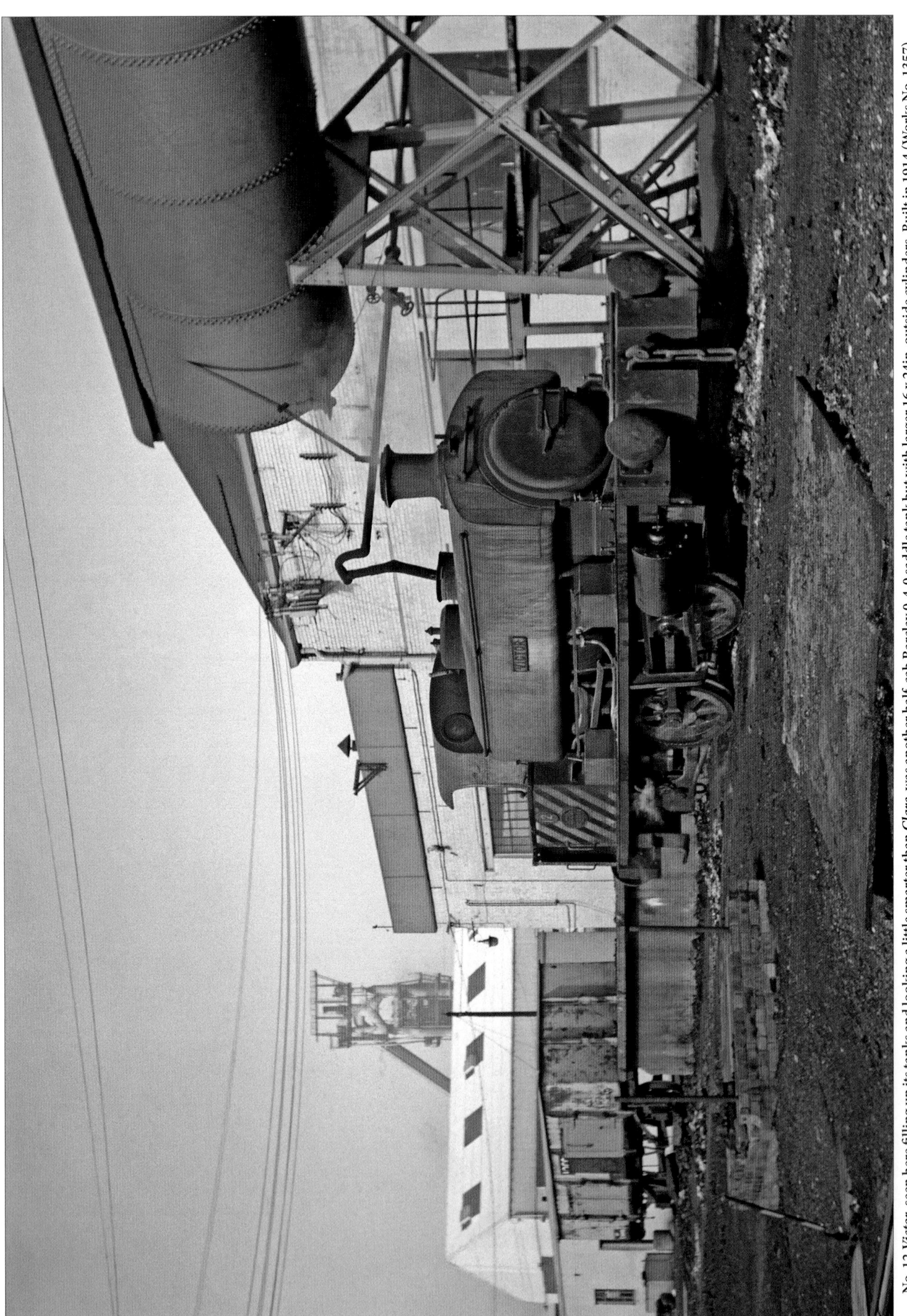

No. 12 *Victor*, seen here filling up its tanks and looking a little smarter than *Clare*, was another half-cab Barclay 0-4-0 saddle tank but with larger 16 x 24in. outside cylinders. Built in 1914 (Works No. 1357) and delivered new to Springvale, it was scrapped in August 1965. *Sunday 30th September 1962*

& Lloyds Ltd, it went on to produce 275,000 tons of steel a year. Stewarts & Lloyds Ltd became part of the British Steel Corporation on nationalisation of the industry in 1967 and it was fully absorbed the following year. The furnace was demolished in October 1980, eighteen months after steel production ended at the site.

Patricia, **Andrew Barclay 16 x 24in. outside cylinder 0-4-0 saddle tank 1842 built in 1924, was also busy about its duties. It, like *Victor,* was delivered new and it was scrapped in October 1965.** ***Sunday 30th September 1962***

At another part of the site on that day, *Anne* was building up a good head of steam. An Andrew Barclay 16 x 24in. outside cylinder 0-4-0 saddle tank built in 1924, Works No. 1841, it was delivered new to Springvale Furnaces in October 1924 and scrapped forty-one years later. ***Sunday 30th September 1962***

Anne was working hard that day. I saw it at work again in April 1965, just six months before it was scrapped in October 1965. Along with *Patricia,* it was one of the last two steam locomotives in service at Springvale. *Sunday 30th September 1962*

Stewarts & Lloyds Bromford Bridge Tube Works, Erdington

The ex-Bromford Tube Co. Ltd works was taken over by Stewarts & Lloyds in 1945. The works exchange sidings were adjacent to Bromford Bridge station, which closed on 28th June 1965, on the ex-Midland Railway line from Birmingham to Derby. There were three steam locomotives at Bromford Bridge Tube Works in the first half of the 1960s but they were all withdrawn and cut up in 1967. They were replaced that year by the last steam locomotive at this works, *Wellingborough No. 3*, a Hawthorn, Leslie & Co. 0-4-0 saddle tank of 1935, which was transferred from Stewarts & Lloyds, Corby, and ex-Oxfordshire Ironstone Rolls-Royce 0-4-0 diesel hydraulic *Barabel*. *Wellingborough No. 3* was scrapped in 1971 leaving rail traffic in the hands of *Barabel* and several other diesel shunters which arrived. The works was closed in 1994.

This Avonside Engine Company locomotive with the Works No. 1777 was an 'SS3' Type 14 x 20in. outside cylinder 0-4-0 saddle tank built in 1917. Seen here early in 1962, it had come to Bromford Bridge from the Chesterfield Tube Co. Ltd, Derbyshire, in 1928. It was scrapped on site in December 1967, just before Stewarts & Lloyds became part of the British Steel Corporation on nationalisation.

Peckett 'W6' Type 14 x 22in. outside cylinder 0-4-0 saddle tank built in 1937, with the confusing Works No. 1936, was also to be seen at the tube works early in 1962. This locomotive had been supplied new to the Bromford Tube Co. Ltd and it was cut up there after thirty years in December 1967.

Three years later, another Peckett, a 'W7' Type 14 x 22in. outside cylinder 0-4-0 saddle tank with the Works No. 2119, was out of steam. This locomotive was built in 1950 and was also supplied new to Bromford Bridge. Like the other two locomotives shown here, it was cut up on site at the end of 1967.
Saturday 10th April 1965

Hodbarrow Haematite Mine and Millom Ironworks

Haematite (iron ore) mining at Hodbarrow had started in 1856 and continued until the mine closed in March 1968. The associated Millom Ironworks, where the Millom & Askam Iron Company had built the first furnaces in 1866, followed on 13th September the same year. The Hodbarrow branch connected the works to the ex-Furness Railway at Millom station. Much of the site was bought by the Royal Society for the Protection of Birds in 1986 and has become the Hodbarrow Local Nature Reserve, a large coastal lagoon and grassland area locally called the 'Slaggy', which is part of the Duddon Estuary SSSI.

Hunslet Engine Company Works No. 299 was built in 1884 and became *Hodbarrow No. 5* at the Hodbarrow iron ore mine at Millom. Seen here already out of service, this locomotive has since been saved and moved to the Statfold Barn Railway to be restored. It is now exhibited there looking much smarter than in the photograph in green livery and carrying the name *Hodbarrow. Sunday 12th September 1965*

Avonside Engine Company Works No. 1563 standing out of steam at Millom Quarries with a neatly boarded up cab side. It is a 12 x 18in. outside cylinder 0-4-0 saddle tank and it was supplied new to John Paton, Pontypool Tinplate Works in South Wales in 1908 where it was named *John Paton*. It was bought by the dealer A.R. Adams and Sons of Newport in January 1933 and sold on to the Hodbarrow Mining Co. at Millom at the end of 1934, where it was renamed *Millom. Sunday 12th September 1965*

Another look at the Avonside Engine Company Works No. 1563 at Millom Quarries. It has been saved from the cutter's torch and moved to the Foxfield Railway for restoration possibly with the name ***John Paton*** once again. *Sunday 12th September 1965*

Millom Ironworks No. 4, a 4WTG built by Sentinel of Shrewsbury in 1955, appeared to be out of action. It carried the worksplate number 9586. This was correct for the cab which had been cannibalised from sister locomotive No. 5 but the rest was, in fact, Works No. 9585. *Sunday 12th September 1965*

Millom Ironworks No. 2 runs light across a level crossing. This Andrew Barclay 16 x 24in. outside cylinder 0-4-0 saddle tank with the Works No. 2334 was built in 1953 and delivered new to the Millom Ironworks. *Sunday 12th September 1965*

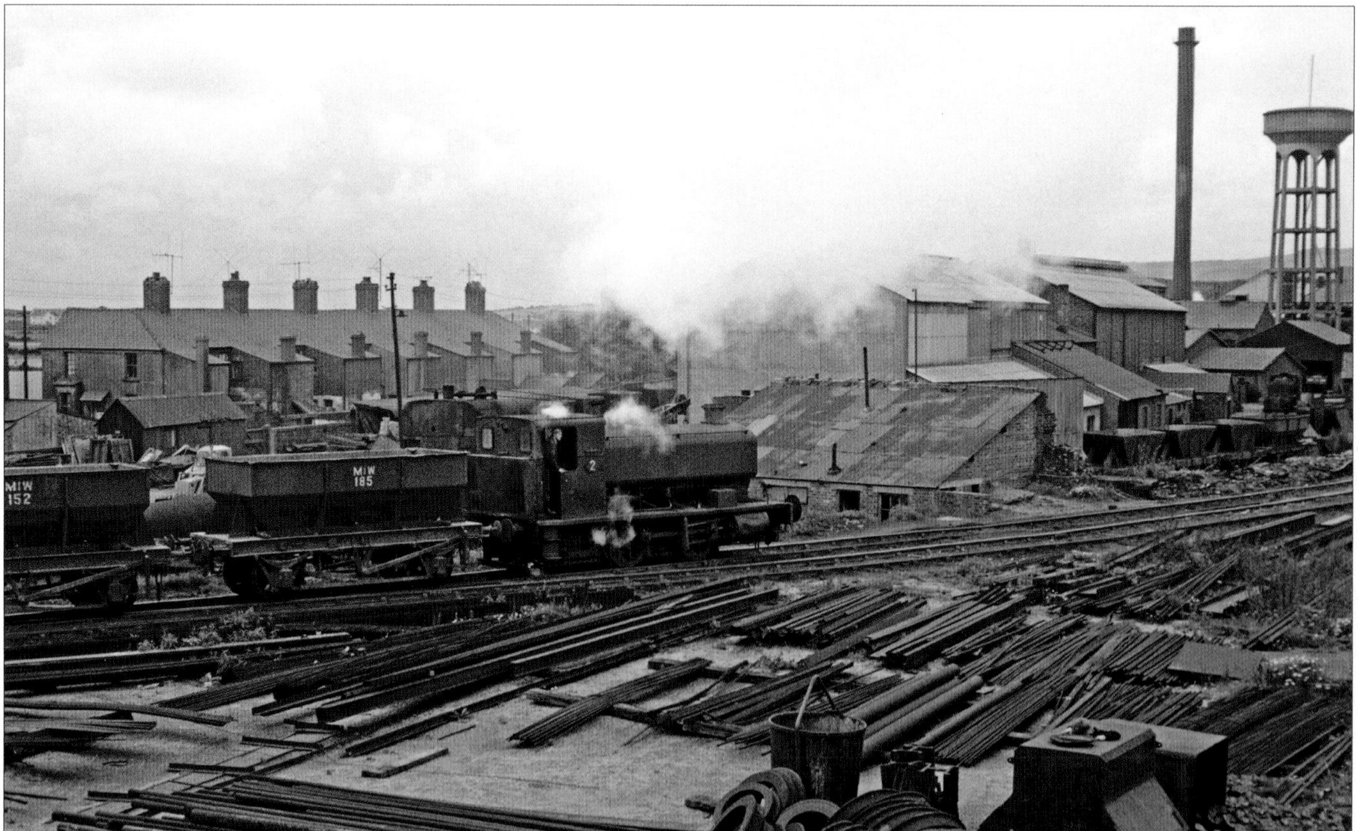

Another look at Millom Ironworks No. 2 at work. No. 2 was scrapped in 1969, the year after the ironworks closed. Sister locomotive No. 1, Andrew Barclay 2333, which was also a Millom Ironworks locomotive is now preserved on the Lakeside & Haverthwaite Railway and has been named *David*.
Sunday 12th September 1965

Chapter 3

National Coal Board
The Warwickshire Coalfield

The collieries using steam locomotive in Warwickshire, in the National Coal Board West Midlands Division area 4, were all situated in the north of the county between Coventry and Tamworth.

Baddesley Colliery, Baxterley

The ex-Baddesley Colliery Co. Ltd Baddesley and Baxterley Pit, which was sunk in 1851, closed in 1979. A memorial in the nave of the local church commemorates those who lost their lives in one of the worst pit disasters in the Midlands when a coal dust explosion in 1882 led to the deaths of 32 men, including the owner William Dugdale of Merevale Hall. Baddesley Sidings were near Atherstone on the ex-London & North Western Railway Trent Valley line between Nuneaton and Tamworth. The colliery line over the A5 to the sidings was closed in 1974 and the mine followed in 1989.

The most exceptional, and probably best known, locomotive in use in the Warwickshire Coalfield at the time was undoubtedly the distinctive 0-4-4-0 *William Francis* at Baddesley Colliery. The engine, which was built by Beyer, Peacock & Co. at their Gorton Foundry in Manchester in 1937, with the Works No. 6841, is seen here approaching the colliery exchange sidings to collect some wagons. *Thursday 2nd January 1964*

After collecting the empty wagons, ***William Francis*** propelled them away from the interchange sidings. Locomotives pulled trains downhill but pushed them up the incline. This locomotive was named after Sir William Francis Dugdale, the son of the founder of the colliery, and it was the third one at the colliery to carry the name. It was one of only a handful, I believe four, of Beyer Garratt locomotives built by Beyer, Peacock for industrial use in the UK. This powerful locomotive, with four 13½ x 20 in. outside cylinders, had 3ft 4in. driving wheels, boiler pressure of 185 lbs and a tractive effort of 30,821lbs. It was useful because of the steeply graded nearly two mile long branch line from the interchange sidings to the colliery in the village of Baxterly which rose about 240ft at an average gradient of 1 in 47. *Thursday 2nd January 1964*

I believe ***William Francis*** was taken out of service in the spring of 1966 and despite apparent initial interest for preservation in Canada it remained in England and went into preservation at Alan Bloom's Bressingham Steam & Gardens near Diss in Norfolk in July 1968. It can now be seen there albeit in a rather different livery. According to Roger E. West in an interesting article in the *Industrial Railway Record* of September 1966, this locomotive leaked so much steam that, in addition to a lookout on the first wagon when trains were propelled uphill, another man had to stand on the locomotive in front of the smokebox to relay any warning! I did not witness this when I photographed ***William Francis*** in January 1964 so it is probable that the leak developed later.

William Francis **propelled the empty wagons back to Baddesley Colliery that day. Apparently, the maximum load for *William Francis* was eighteen 16-ton mineral wagons.** ***Thursday 2nd January 1964***

Baddesley No.1 **catches the sun as it backs light over the A5 towards Baddesley Colliery exchange sidings. *William Francis* can be seen behind. *Baddesley No. 1* was an 18 x 26in. inside cylinder Hunslet Engine Co. 'Austerity' 0-6-0 saddle tank built for the War Department in 1943 with the Works No. 2859. Originally WD No. 75010, it entered service at the Royal Engineers Long Marston depot before transfer to the Longmoor Military Railway the following year. This locomotive was bought for Griff Colliery in March 1948. It was of interest because in June 1959 it was one of the first British locomotives to be fitted for tests with a Giesel ejector in place of the usual chimney. It went to Wm Bush Ltd of Alfreton for scrap in February 1968.** ***Thursday 2nd January 1964***

A second Hunslet 'Austerity' Type 18 x 26in. inside cylinder 0-6-0 saddle tank at Baddesley was built in 1953 by Robert Stephenson and Hawthorns with the Works No. 7752. Named ***Warwickshire***, it had entered service new at Kingsbury Colliery and then, after a short spell at Birch Coppice, it was transferred to Baddesley early in 1957. It was rebuilt by W.G. Bagnall when only nine years old, just before this photograph was taken. A diesel generator which powered a mechanical stoker can be seen mounted on the front of the frames. This had been fitted during the rebuild but it seems that it was noisy and unpopular with the locomen and the assembly was removed the following year. Like ***Baddesley No. 1***, it was sent for scrap to Wm Bush Ltd of Alfreton in February 1968.
Sunday 8th April 1962

Birch Coppice Colliery, Dordon

The ex-Morris & Shaw Ltd Birch Coppice Colliery, earlier called Hall End Colliery, was linked by a short line to the ex-Midland Railway Kingsbury branch which was in turn connected with the ex-Midland Railway main line between Hampton-in-Arden and Tamworth, just north of the now closed Kingsbury station. The colliery closed on 29th November 1986 although rail traffic had ended several months earlier.

The appropriately named *Birch Coppice* was a Hunslet Engine Co. 0-6-0 saddle tank built in 1929 with the Works No. 1637. This engine had been delivered new to Morris and Shaw Ltd, the then owners of Birch Coppice Colliery. I saw it hard at work on the short branch linking the colliery with the ex-Midland Railway Kingsbury branch. This locomotive was withdrawn from service and cut up by Cashmore's of Great Bridge the following year.

John Robert, a 16 x 24in. outside cylinder 0-6-0 saddle tank built by Manning, Wardle of Leeds in 1916 with the Works No. 1891, working at Birch Coppice Colliery. It had been transferred from Baddesley Colliery, after a stay at the Ansley Central Workshops, in September 1962. The locomotive had originally been named *Merevale* after Merevale Hall, the Dugdale family home. John Robert Stratford Dugdale was the younger grandson of the founder of Baddesley Colliery. It was cut up at some time in late 1965 or early 1966. *Friday 9th April 1965*

Seen here, *Coventry No. 3* was a Peckett 'OX1' Type 16 x 24in. outside cylinder 0-6-0 saddle tank (Works No. 1700) and, as the name suggests, it originally worked at Coventry Colliery, Keresley, where it was supplied new in 1925. It had been transferred to Birch Coppice Colliery just a few days before this photograph was taken. Behind it is Avonside Engine Co. *Empress. Coventry No. 3* was scrapped at the colliery at the end of 1970. *Friday 9th April 1965*

Arley Colliery

The ex-Arley Colliery Co. Ltd mine, where exploration for coal had started in 1901, was situated near the ex-Midland Railway line from Birmingham to Nuneaton and the interchange was at Arley Sidings. It closed on 29th March 1968.

Empress, **an Avonside Engine Co. 'SS' Type 14 x 20in. outside cylinder 0-4-0 saddle tank built in 1911 with the Works No. 1591, was out of steam here. It was transferred to Birch Coppice Colliery in February 1964 where I saw it two months later. On both occasions it was out of use. Perhaps it was not really powerful enough for more than light shunting duties. It was cut up at Birch Coppice Colliery in March 1966.** ***Sunday 8th April 1962***

Coventry No. 4, **a Peckett 'OX1' Type 16 x 24in. outside cylinder 0-6-0 saddle tank built in 1927 with the Works No. 1745, was hard at work at Arley Colliery. The 'OX1' Type had 3ft10in. driving wheels and were very suitable for working branch line trains as they were larger than those usually found on Peckett locomotives. (The ubiquitous 'W5', 'W6' and 'W7' Types had 3ft 2½in. wheels). As its name suggests, this locomotive had been transferred from Coventry Colliery where it had been supplied new to the colliery's owners, the Warwickshire Coal Company. It returned to Coventry in 1968 but it was scrapped at the end of the following year.** ***Thursday 2nd April 1964***

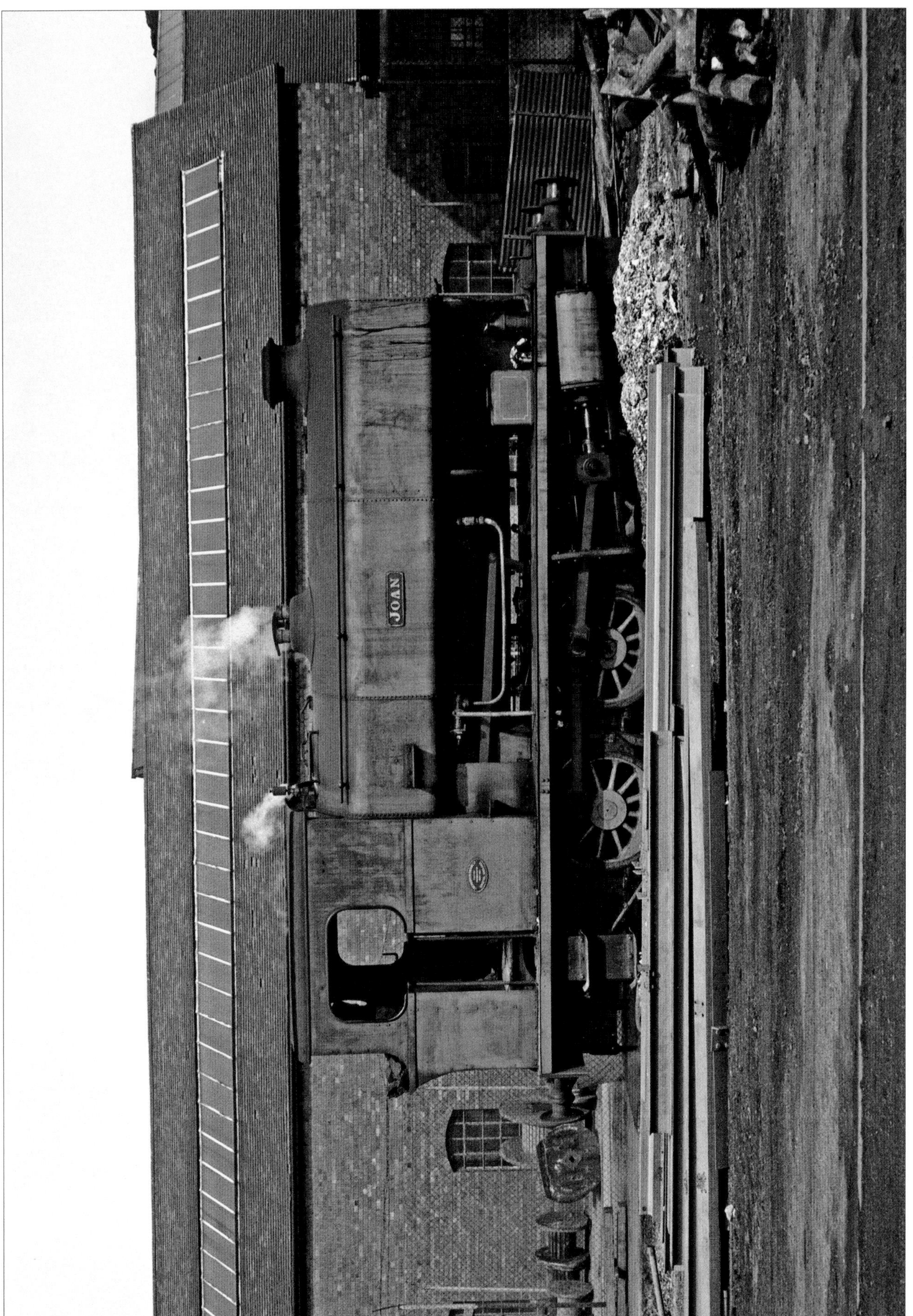

It is interesting to compare *Empress* with this later, and much larger, Avonside Engine Co. product seen at work at Arley Colliery. *Joan* was a 16 x 24in. outside cylinder 0-6-0 saddle tank built in 1932 with the Works No. 2048. It was transferred to Newdigate Colliery six months after production at Arley ended on 30th March 1968 but was out of use there soon afterwards. I saw it at Newdigate looking rather sad for itself with its nameplates removed on Tuesday 5th August 1969. It was finally disposed of at the end of 1971. *Friday 9th April 1965*

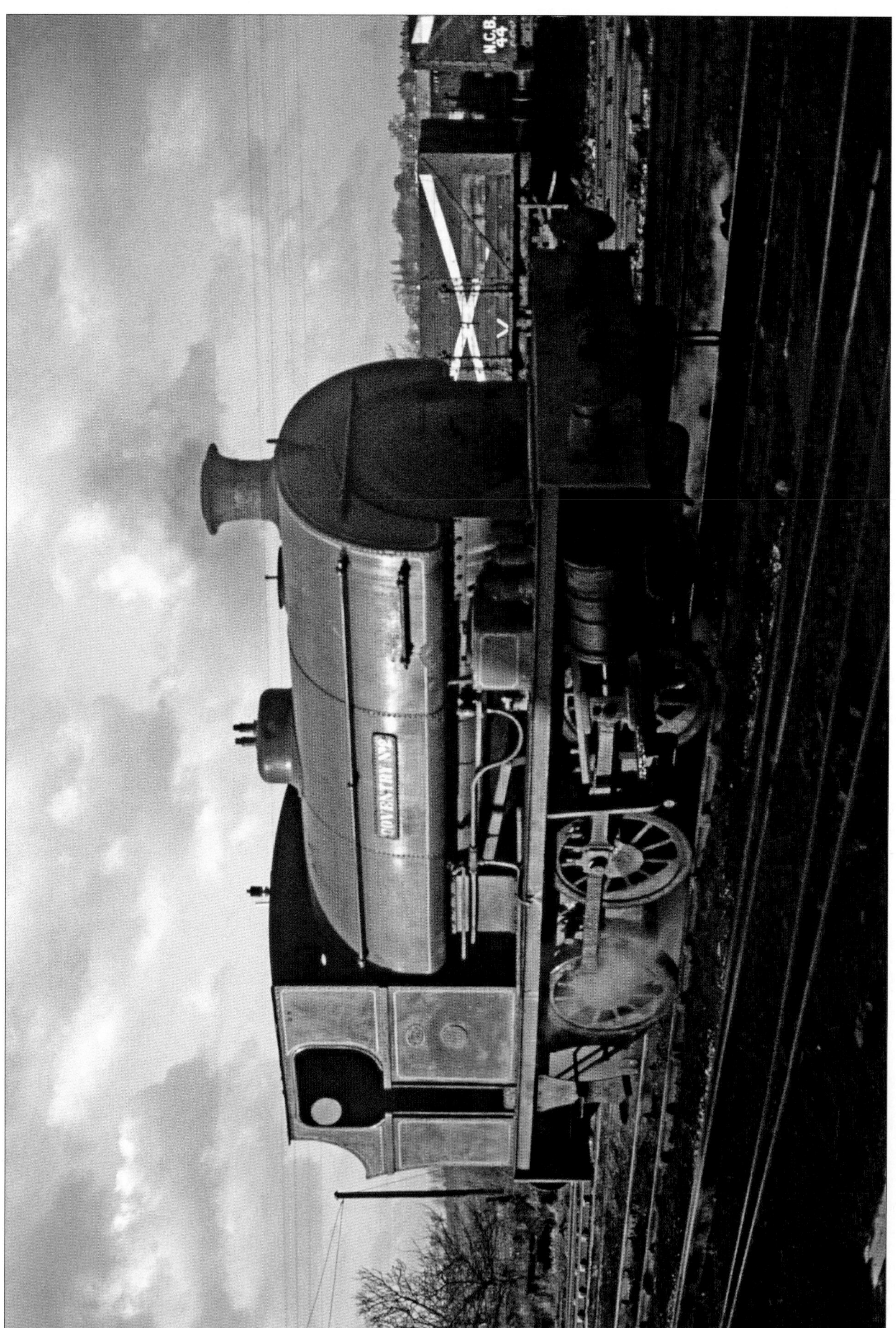

A second ex-Coventry Colliery locomotive in action at Arley was *Coventry No. 2*. It was also a Peckett 'OX1' Type 16 x 24in. outside cylinder 0-6-0 saddle tank, built in 1924 with the Works No. 1662. Like *Coventry No. 4*. it had been delivered new to the Warwickshire Coal Co. Ltd Coventry Colliery and was transferred to Arley after overhaul by Andrew Barclay in 1963. It was returned to Coventry Colliery in the September after this photo was taken but was scrapped there by T.W. Ward in September 1969. *Thursday 28th December 1967*

This Avonside Engine Company of Bristol 16 x 24in. outside cylinder 0-6-0 saddle tank, built in 1922 with the Works No. 1883, did not carry an NCB name or number. It had large 4ft 0in. wheels and is seen here at Arley Colliery. Delivered new to Haunchwood Colliery in North Warwickshire, it had moved to Arley on the closure of that pit. It was later transferred to Newdigate Colliery and then Baddesley Colliery. Although an Avonside product, it had been given a new Andrew Barclay boiler in 1950 and a Hunslet inner firebox later on. After transfer to Newdigate Colliery in 1968 and then, the following year, to Baddesley Colliery and withdrawal from service, AE 1883 was purchased by the Dinting Railway Centre where it arrived during July 1975. It is now at the Ribble Steam Railway at Preston. *Thursday 28th December 1967*

Coventry Colliery, Keresley

The ex-Warwickshire Coal Co. Ltd Coventry Colliery, Keresley, began operating in 1917 and was in full production by 1923. It was closed in October 1991 but was later sold to Coal Investments Ltd and reopened for a couple of years before finally closing in August 1996. It is now the site of the Pro-Logis Industrial Park. A two mile long branch line connected the colliery to the ex-London and North Western Railway line from Coventry to Nuneaton at Three Spires Junction, near the now closed Foleshill station, in Coventry. After the colliery was closed the line was relaid to serve the industrial estate.

Of particular interest in the 1960s were three '1500' Class locomotives bought from British Railways. These were 0-6-0 pannier tanks designed by Frederick Hawksworth for the Great Western Railway but, following nationalisation in 1948, they were actually built by the Western Region of British Railways the following year. There were only ever ten of the class and they were intended for heavy shunting duties so they were well suited to colliery work. Of course they held a special attraction for GWR enthusiasts after the end of Western Region steam. The pannier tanks remained at Keresley Colliery until 1970 when they were no longer required by the NCB as they had been replaced by diesel shunters. Having neatly rounded off steam operation in the 1960s decade, all three locomotives went to the Severn Valley Railway where No. 1501 is still based. Unfortunately, No's 1502 and 1509 were used solely to provide spares for the restoration of 1501 and the remaining parts were scrapped at Cashmore's of Great Bridge in October 1970. There had even been an earlier ex-GWR locomotive in use at this colliery. This was *Coventry No. 5*, a Sharp, Stewart 0-6-0 side tank locomotive built in 1888. It was originally Barry Railway No. 1 and later GWR No. 699 before it arrived at Coventry Colliery in 1933. It is a great shame that this historic and attractive locomotive, which I regret I never saw, was scrapped when the pannier tanks arrived in 1962.

Western Region 0-6-0 pannier tanks No's 1509, 1502 and 1501, withdrawn from British Railways service wait at Swindon Works in what looked like a scrap line. No. 1509 even had 'COND' and 'SCRAP' chalked on it. They had a lucky escape, however, as all three were sent to Andrew Barclay Ltd of Kilmarnock to be overhauled, because they had been earmarked to go to NCB Keresley Colliery. No's 1501 and 1502 arrived in 1962 followed by No. 1509 the next year. With a tractive effort of 22,515 lbs, and classified as '4F' by BR, they were thought eminently suitable to haul trains on the two mile long branch line. *Tuesday 4th April 1961*

No. 1501 in action at Keresley Colliery. It was built at Swindon in July 1949 and it spent its British Railways working life at Old Oak Common (81A) and Southall (81C) motive power depots. It had been one of the first of the class to be withdrawn by BR, in January 1961. *Monday 9th August 1965*

No. 1501 sets off along the branch at Keresley Colliery. *Friday 9th April 1965*

The last of the ten '1500' Class pannier tanks, No. 1509, had a slightly different life. It was also built at Swindon and it was outshopped in September 1949. It then spent its working life in South Wales, at Newport Pill (86B) and Newport Ebbw Junction (86A) sheds, before being withdrawn by British Railways in August 1959. It seen here in action at Keresley. *Monday 9th August 1965*

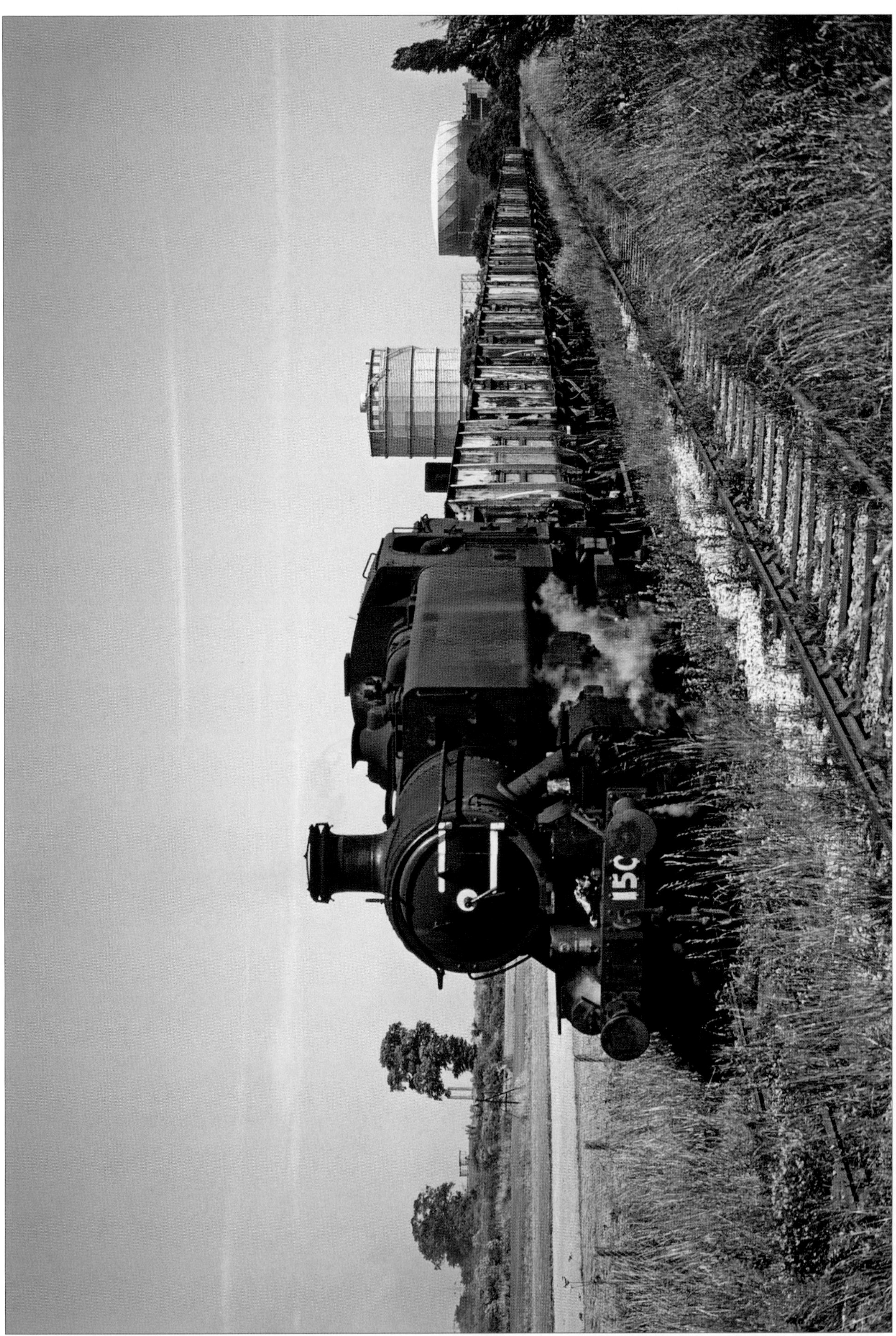

Despite losing its cabside number plates and looking rather neglected, No. 1502 was still showing why these powerful locomotives were so suitable for the branch line at Keresley Colliery. It had been outshopped from Swindon in July 1949 and it spent its BR working life allocated to Old Oak Common (81A) and Didcot (81E) sheds and was withdrawn from British Railways service in January 1961. The gasholders behind were at Foleshill gas works, now the site of the Ricoh Arena with a stadium which was formerly used by Coventry City Football Club and now by Wasps Rugby Union Football Club, an exhibition hall, a shopping centre and a hotel. *Friday 4th July 1969*

Seen here towards to the end of its working life is No. 1502, on duty at Keresley, though by this time trains along the branch were often worked by diesel shunters from the Coventry Homefire Plant and two new Hunslet Engine Co. 0-6-0 diesel hydraulic shunters would arrive at the end of the year.
Thursday 7th August 1969

Coventry Homefire Plant

The controversial Coventry Homefire Smokeless Coal Plant was situated next to Keresley Colliery. Local residents suspected that, ironically, in producing smokeless fuel briquettes it was polluting the local environment and seriously affecting the health of those who worked there. It started production in 1967 and outlived the colliery, finally closing in 2000.

Just after the development of the Coventry Homefire Plant had begun, I saw HE Works No. 3885 there. It was a Hunslet Engine Company 'Austerity' 18 x 26in. inside cylinder 0-6-0 saddle tank built in 1944 with the Works No. 3163. Originally War Department 75113, then WD No. 132, it was delivered to the Bicester depot and then relocated to other depots before returning to Bicester where it was given the name *Sapper* from 1959 to 1961. It was then sold to Hunslet where it was rebuilt with the Works No. 3885 and loaned to the NCB at Coventry three months before this photograph was taken. It was returned to Hunslet in May the following year along with a second 'Austerity' Type built by W.G. Bagnall in 1945 (Works No. 2774 but rebuilt in 1965 as Hunslet Works No. 3893) which apparently arrived a few weeks after I was there. Next it went to the NCB Walkden workshops, Greater Manchester, where it was named *Alison*. Later, in 1970, it went to the notorious NCB Gresford Colliery, Wrexham, site of one of Britain's worst coal mining disasters, and then to Lancashire at Bold Colliery, in 1974, where it was renamed *Joseph*. Notable as one of the last steam engines operating in the UK, it went to the Chatterley Whitfield Mining Museum in Staffordshire in 1986, and then to the South Devon Railway. It is now based on the East Lancashire Railway and has worked at Peak Rail and the Avon Valley Railway as WD No. 132 *Sapper* once again. *Monday 9th August 1965*

Haunchwood Colliery, Nuneaton

The ex-Haunchwood Collieries Co. Ltd Haunchwood Colliery was situated alongside the ex-Midland Railway line from Whitacre to Nuneaton at Tunnel Pit Sidings between the now closed Stockingford station and Arley Tunnel. The colliery closed on 25th March 1967.

The seventy-four year old ***Good Luck*** did not appear to be living up to its name as it lay out of service at Haunchwood Colliery. Built by the Hunslet Engine Co. in 1890 with the Works No. 498, this 13 x 18in. inside cylinder 0-6-0 saddle tank had received a new boiler in the early 1950s when working at Griff Colliery, to where it had been supplied new. It was transferred to Haunchwood Colliery in September 1962 but apparently it was not really powerful enough for its new tasks so the hard work passed on to a much younger Hunslet product, ***Haunchwood Colliery No. 1. Good Luck*** was scrapped by Cashmore's of Great Bridge in June 1966. ***Thursday 2nd April 1964***

Haunchwood Colliery No. 1 was a Hunslet 'Austerity' Type 18 x 26in. inside cylinder 0-6-0 saddle tank built by the Hunslet Engine Co. in 1955 with the Works No. 3828. It was supplied new to Haunchwood Colliery where this photograph was taken. It was still there when the colliery closed on 25th March 1967 but it went to Cashmore's of Great Bridge for scrap in the autumn. ***Thursday 2nd April 1964***

Newdigate Colliery, Bedworth

Coal production at the ex-Newdigate Collieries Co. Ltd mine near Bedworth started in 1901. The colliery was connected to the ex-London & North Western Railway main line from Coventry to Nuneaton just to the south of Bedworth station by a two mile branch line. There was also a siding to a wharf on the Newdigate Colliery branch of the Coventry Canal. The colliery was closed in February 1982 although rail traffic had ceased the previous June.

No.4, a Peckett 'X2' Type 16 x 22in. inside cylinder 0-6-0 saddle tank, was built in 1933 with the Works No. 1787. It was apparently already out of use at Newdigate Colliery when photographed. Delivered in May 1933, it was scrapped towards the end of 1971. *Tuesday 5th August 1969*

Looking very smart at work at Newdigate Colliery, Bedworth, *Coventry No. 1* was, and fortunately still is, a handsome North British Locomotive Co. Ltd 18 x 26in. inside cylinder 0-6-0 side tank engine. It was one of a pair built in 1939 to a Neilson, Reid design, with the Works No. 24564. The other one remained in Scotland. At the time it was the only side tank locomotive working in the NCB West Midlands Division Area 4. *Coventry No. 1* had been supplied new to the Warwickshire Coal Co. Ltd and allocated to their Coventry Colliery at Keresley, as its name testifies. After an overhaul which included a new boiler at the NCB workshops at Ansley, it was transferred to Newdigate Colliery in October 1963 where it was restricted to the colliery yard because it had flangeless centre driving wheels. *Friday 9th April 1965*

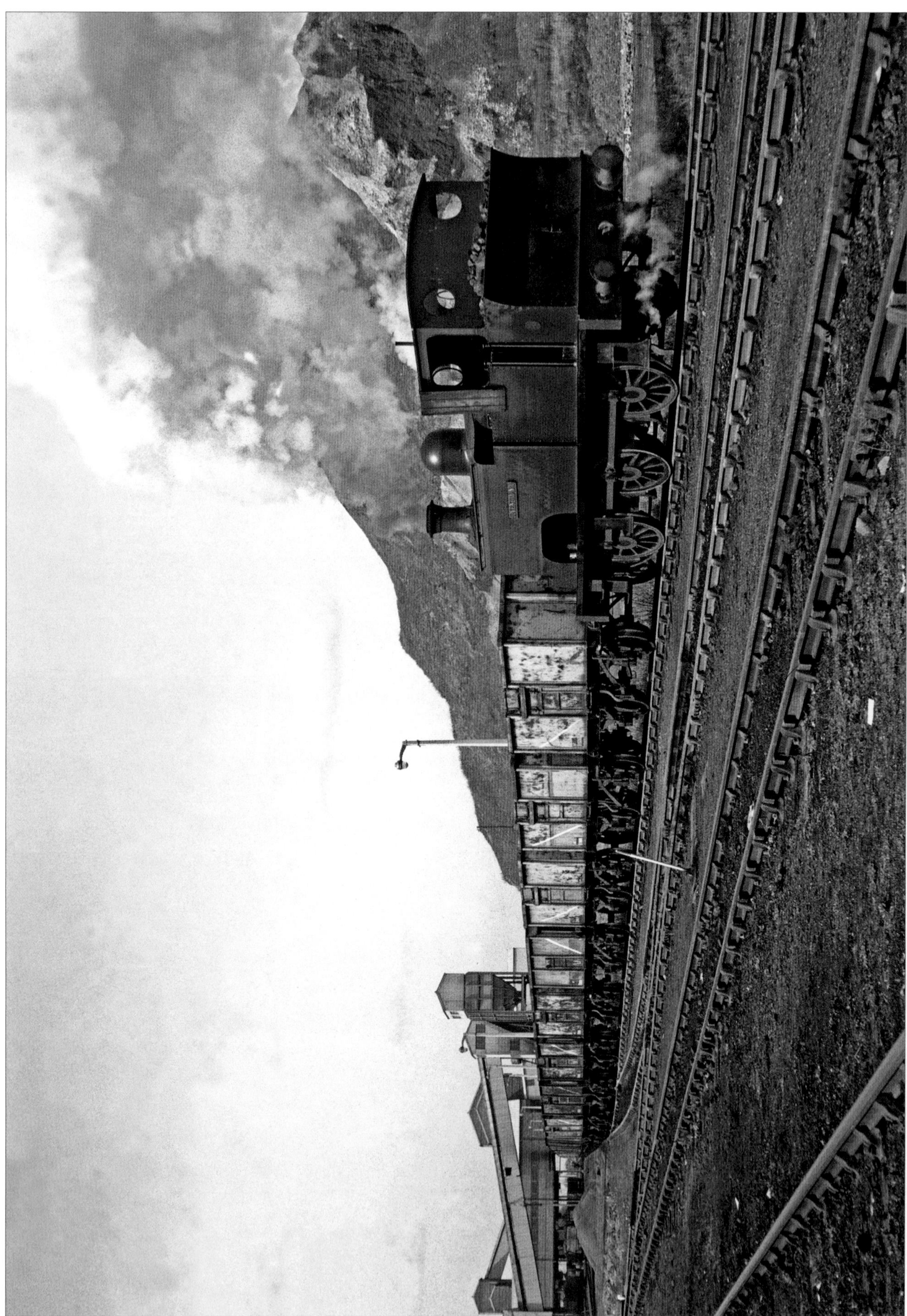

Shortly after this photograph was taken, *Coventry No. 1* was transferred to Haunchwood Colliery but it was returned to Newdigate in June 1967. When made redundant by diesels, it was fortunately sold for preservation to the Quainton Railway Society and moved to their site at Quainton Road station in Buckinghamshire in January 1971 where it has been used to haul passenger trains. More recently, it has been given the identity of ***Thomas the Tank Engine*** and has been hired out to other railways. *Friday 9th April 1965*

No. 3, a Peckett 'X2' Type 16 x 22in. inside cylinder 0-6-0 saddle tank built in 1922 with the Works No. 1586 at work at Newdigate Colliery. *Monday 9th August 1965*

No. 3, the Peckett 0-6-0 saddle tank built in 1922 with the Works No. 1586, had to work hard to raise the empty wagons along the steeply graded siding from the Newdigate Colliery arm of the Coventry Canal towards the colliery. *Thursday 28th December 1967*

No. 3 was alongside the Newdigate Colliery arm of the Coventry Canal near Bedworth on that very cold Thursday. All the wagon side doors were open so presumably coal had been discharged. The bridge behind carried the ex-London & North Western Railway Coventry to Nuneaton main line. The structure beyond the wagons was a cover which could be moved along its own rails which can be seen on either side of the running rails. *Thursday 28th December 1967*

A closer look at No. 3 back at Newdigate Colliery by the water pipe at the engine shed after its trip to the canal wharf. It spent its entire life at Newdigate until it was withdrawn and scrapped on site in 1968. *Thursday 28th December 1967*

Newdigate Colliery No. 1 **was an 'Austerity' Type Hunslet Engine Co. 18 x 26in. inside cylinder 0-6-0 saddle tank built in 1956 with the Works No. 3841. It was delivered new to Newdigate Colliery where it was in action here. This was the day that the Beatles'** ***Ticket to Ride*** **was released.** ***Friday 9th April 1965***

Newdigate Colliery No. 1 **poses for a photograph four months later. It was sent to Cashmore's of Great Bridge for scrap in October 1968.**
Monday 9th August 1965

There were three attractive locomotives at Pooley Hall colliery. Two were Peckett 0-4-0 saddle tanks. The older one, *Kia Ora*, was built in 1912, with the Works No. 1173, and rebuilt in 1954. It was a Peckett 'W5' Type with 14 x 20in. outside cylinders. *Kia Ora* comes from the Maori greeting meaning 'Hello!' or 'Welcome!'. Pooley Hall closed exactly one week after this picture was taken and *Kia Ora* was cut up in June 1966. *Friday 9th April 1965*

Pooley Hall Colliery, Polesworth

Coal was first extracted at Pooley Hall at Dordon around 1850 and the colliery there was established in 1897. After nationalisation this ex-Pooley Hall Colliery Co. Ltd mine was also called North Warwickshire Colliery when amalgamated with other collieries in 1951. The rail link was with the ex-London and North Western Railway main line between Polesworth and Tamworth.

The colliery closed on 16th April 1965, Good Friday, and it is now the site of the Pooley Country Park and there is a heritage centre where you can find out about the mining history of the area. I have read that Pooley Hall was the first coal mine in the country to install pit-head baths!

Kia Ora's **younger sister** ***Kapai*****, built by Peckett in 1920 with the Works No. 1532, was also a 'W5' Type 14 x 20in. outside cylinder 0-4-0 saddle tank. Seen here working at Pooley Hall Colliery, its name was also of New Zealand origin from the Maori expression for 'Good!' or 'Well done!'.** *Thursday 2nd April 1964*

The third locomotive was the venerable Victorian age ***Cowburn***, a Hunslet Engine Co. outside cylinder 0-4-0 saddle tank built in 1891 with the Works No. 544. It had originally been used by a contractor building the Midland Railway Hope Valley line between Manchester and Sheffield and it owed its name to one of the tunnels there. It had, however, been at Pooley Hall since 1896. On a very wet Friday, the driver of ***Kapai*** very kindly hauled ***Cowburn*** out of the engine shed for me to photograph it. The colliery closed exactly one week after this and, no longer needed, both ***Cowburn*** and ***Kapai*** ended their days early in 1966 at Bird's Commercial Motors scrap yard at Long Marston. *Friday 9th April 1965*

Two real veterans, the 96-years-old No. 1 *Marquis* and another nineteenth century locomotive, No. 3 (right), at rest at Grove Colliery having already been taken out of service. Both were moved to Cannock Central Workshops within few days where No. 3 was cut up a couple of months later after some parts had been cannibalised for use on a sister locomotive. No. 3 was a Peckett 'X' Type 16 x 22in. inside cylinder 0-6-0 saddle tank with 3ft 10in. wheels built in 1895 with the Works No. 618. It had been delivered new to William Harrison Ltd at Grove Colliery and it remained there for all its working life.
Sunday 24 March 1963

Chapter 4

National Coal Board
The Cannock Chase Coalfield

Cannock Chase Central Workshops

Locomotive maintenance for the Cannock Chase area was carried out at the ex-Cannock Chase Colliery Co. Ltd Cannock Chase Central Workshops which was situated next to the company's No. 3 pit and opened in 1924. For some reason the workshop building was locally called 'Wembley'. The colliery stopped production in 1959 because the coal reserves were poor. The workshops were connected to the Cannock Chase collieries rail network until that closed in 1962 but locomotives continued to be serviced there for about three more years. They did not finally close until 1990.

Ex-War Department WD No. 75070 was an 18 x 26in. inside cylinder Hunslet 'Austerity' Type 0-6-0 saddle tank built in 1943 by Robert Stephenson and Hawthorns Ltd at the North Banks Works in Newcastle-upon-Tyne with the Works No. 7106. It first served at the Kineton Munitions Depot in Warwickshire until it was acquired by Cannock Chase Collieries, Chasetown, from the War Department in December 1946. It had clearly just been overhauled when seen here at the Cannock Chase Central Workshops. It was transferred to Littleton Colliery in April 1963, just four weeks after this photograph was taken, where it became No. 8. It was scrapped at that colliery in 1968. *Sunday 24th March 1963*

ABOVE: No. 1 *Marquis* was a 17 x 22in. inside cylinder 0-6-0 saddle tank which had been acquired new by the Cannock and Rugeley Colliery Co. Ltd in 1867. It was then based at the Rawnsley Shed on the Cannock Chase Railway until it was transferred to Grove Colliery in January 1962. It is seen here withdrawn from service and waiting for disposal. Sadly, it was scrapped at the Cannock Central Workshops in May 1964. *Marquis*, named after the Marquis of Anglesey, the local landowner, was a particularly interesting locomotive because it was a rare Lilleshall Company Ltd of Oakengates, Shropshire, product. This company only constructed locomotives between 1862 and 1888. *Sunday 24th March 1963*

Grove Colliery, Wyrley

Grove Colliery, which was formerly owned by William Harrison Ltd, was sunk in 1870. In 1930 there was an explosion which killed fourteen miners. Even after extraction ended at Grove Colliery, coal from the adjacent Wyrley No. 3 Colliery with which it was linked continued to be washed, screened and distributed from there. The facilities were closed in June 1963 and demolition began the following year. It had a rail connection to the ex-London & North Western Railway at Norton Branch Junction near Pelsall in Staffordshire.

LEFT: *Conduit No. 3*, a Manning, Wardle 'O' Type 15 x 22in. inside cylinder 0-6-0 saddle tank built in 1890 with the Works No. 1180, was inside the engine shed at Grove Colliery that day. Acquired new for Conduit Colliery, it was transferred to Littleton Colliery before 1910. It was rebuilt by Manning, Wardle in 1920. In 1949 it was moved to West Cannock Colliery, then, after a rebuild with parts of *Conduit No. 4* (Manning, Wardle Works No. 1326) in 1960 or 1961, to Grove Colliery. Finally, in July 1963, after this photograph was taken, it went to Rawnsley Colliery where it was cut up in December 1964. *Sunday 24th March 1963*

Littleton Colliery, Huntington

The ex-Littleton Collieries Ltd mine was situated between Cannock and Stafford and was linked to the ex-London & North Western Railway main line from Wolverhampton to Stafford at exchange sidings near Penkridge by a steeply graded four mile branch. The last official steam working was in February 1978. Littleton Colliery did not fully close until December 1993 and part of the site has become the Littleton Leisure Park.

Holly Bank No. 3 **out of steam at Littleton Colliery. This Hunslet Engine Co. 16 x 22in. inside cylinder 0-6-0 saddle tank was built in 1924 with the Works No. 1451 and was supplied new to Hilton Main & Holly Bank Collieries Ltd where it obtained its name. It was transferred from Holly Bank Colliery to Littleton Colliery in January 1959 and moved again to Granville Colliery in June 1966 where it was soon out of use and cut up in July 1968.** ***Holly Bank No. 3*** **is today remembered in the guise of a similar but more recent Hunslet locomotive,** ***Darfield No. 1,*** **which has taken on its identity at the Chasewater Railway.**
Sunday 24th March 1963

No. 6 seen stabled on the left in the locomotive shed at Littleton Colliery. This 'Hunslet Austerity' 18 x 26in. inside cylinder 0-6-0 saddle tank was originally War Department No. 71483 built by Robert Stephenson & Hawthorns Ltd in 1945 with the Works No. 7292. It had arrived at Littleton Colliery in May 1947 and was scrapped on site there in October 1970. Next to it, on the right, was ***Littleton No. 5,*** **a Manning, Wardle 18 x 24in. inside cylinder 0-6-0 saddle tank built in 1922 with the Works No. 2018 and supplied new to Littleton Collieries Ltd.** *Sunday 24th March 1963*

The following year, ***Littleton No. 5*** **was out of steam in the yard. Apparently it was the largest locomotive that Manning, Wardle built and was particularly suited for the steeply graded colliery line to the exchange sidings. When withdrawn from service in 1972, made redundant by diesel locomotives, it went to the Foxfield Railway, Staffordshire, and then to the Great Central Railway at Loughborough in Leicestershire. Since 1980 it is to be found at the Avon Valley Railway at Bitton near Bristol.** ***Saturday 11th January 1964***

Carol Ann No. 1 was a Hunslet Engine Co. 16 x 22in. inside cylinder 0-6-0 saddle tank built in 1936 with the Works No. 1821. It was in the yard at Littleton Colliery when photographed here but not in use that day. It was originally delivered new to Hilton Main and Holly Bank Collieries Ltd and named *Carol Ann No. 5*. It was transferred from Holly Bank Colliery to Littleton Colliery in 1959 where, its service no longer required, it was scrapped on site by Thos W. Ward Ltd in August 1966. *Saturday 11th January 1964*

Cannock Chase Railway Rawnsley Shed and Cannock Wood Colliery

The ex-Cannock & Rugeley Colliery Co. Rawnsley Engine Shed served the Cannock Chase Railway which provided the link between a number of collieries and the ex-London & North Western Railway near Hednesford on the Cannock to Rugeley line. The engine shed closed in February 1965 and locomotives were stabled at a new one at the nearby Cannock Wood Colliery until that mine closed in June 1973.

A particularly interesting locomotive at Cannock Wood Colliery was No. 5 ***Beaudesert.*** This was a Fox, Walker 'B' Class 13 x 20in. outside cylinder 0-6-0 saddle tank built in 1875 with the Works No. 266 which had been acquired new by Cannock & Rugeley Colliery Co. Ltd. Eighty-eight years later, in 1963, someone had repainted the buffer beam and works plate but ***Beaudesert*** was withdrawn around the time this photograph was taken and was cut up by T. Hill at Chasetown in June the following year. Fox, Walker & Company's Atlas Engine Works in Bristol was taken over by Thomas Peckett in 1880 to become Peckett & Sons, Atlas Engine Works. *Sunday 24th March 1963*

Inside the Cannock Wood Rawnsley Engine Shed that day there was a remarkable sight. This was No. 9 *Cannock Wood* and it was the last survivor of a class of eighty London, Brighton & South Coast Railway 'E1' Class 0-6-0 tank engines designed by William Stroudley. This 17 x 24in. inside cylinder 0-6-0 side tank locomotive was built at the LB&SCR Brighton Works in 1877 with the number 110 and named ***Burgundy***. It passed to the Southern Railway and became B110 at the grouping of 1923 and was then sold to the Cannock & Rugeley Colliery Company in 1927. It was still carrying the pre National Coal Board nationalisation letters C.R.C. (Cannock & Rugeley Collieries) on its tank sides when it was withdrawn from service in 1963, around the time this photograph was taken, and saved from the cutter's torch by the Railway Preservation Society.
Sunday 24th March 1963

The following year, No. 9 *Cannock Wood* had arrived at the Railway Preservation Society site at Hednesford in Staffordshire. In 1978 it was sold to members of the East Somerset Railway at Cranmore where it became No. 110 once again. It is now to be found on the Isle of Wight Railway where it has been given the identity of W2 *Yarmouth*, a locomotive of the same class which once worked on the Island. *Saturday January 11th 1964*

Walsall Wood Colliery

The ex-Walsall Wood Colliery Co. Ltd mine had closed on 30th October 1964, six months before this photograph was taken, because the extraction of coal there was no longer considered economically viable. The rail interchanges were on the ex-Midland Railway Aldridge to Brownhills branch, which closed in 1962, and, via a just under two mile long colliery line to the ex-London & North Western Railway Walsall to Lichfield line at Ryder's Hayes Crossing, north of Penshall.

Tony*, a 16 x 24in. outside cylinder 0-6-0 saddle tank built by Hawthorn, Leslie in 1921 with the Works No. 3460, outside and clearly withdrawn from service at Walsall Wood Colliery. Its coupling rods, piston rods, nameplates and works plates had already been removed and the cutters' torches would begin their work the following month. *Tony* had been supplied second-hand to T.A. Hawkins & Sons at Cannock Old Coppice Colliery from Ritson & Sons Ltd Preston Colliery at North Shields in Northumberland via the dealer Geo. Cohen, Sons & Co. Ltd in 1927. It was transferred to Walsall Wood in 1959. *Thursday 22nd April 1965

Despite the fact that Walsall Wood Colliery had closed in the previous October, an unnamed Andrew Barclay 16 x 24in. outside cylinder 0-4-0 saddle tank, built in 1948 with the Works No. 2247, was still in action there. *Thursday 22nd April 1965*

Andrew Barclay Works No. 2247 was presumably involved in some final tidying up as it was scrapped the following month, in May 1965. This locomotive was acquired new for Chasetown Colliery but had also worked at Coppice Colliery, Grove Colliery, Mid Cannock Colliery, and Hamstead Colliery as well as Walsall Wood Colliery. *Thursday 22nd April 1965*

West Cannock No. 5 Colliery, Hednesford

The ex-West Cannock Colliery Co. Ltd mine, also earlier known as Brindley Heath Colliery, was connected to the ex-London & North Western Railway Cannock to Rugeley line opposite the Hednesford No. 3 signal box just north of Hednesford station. Rail working with a diesel locomotive continued until the end of 1977 and the colliery finally closed in 1982.

Stafford, **an attractive Hudswell, Clarke & Co. '24T' 15 x 20in. inside cylinder 0-6-0 side tank locomotive built in 1889 (Works No. 319), out of use at West Cannock Colliery. It was employed in the construction of Immingham Docks and was then bought from a dealer by the War Department in 1915 for service on the Cannock Chase Military Railway. There it was given the number 4094. When no longer needed after the First World War, it was sold to West Cannock Colliery Co. Ltd where it was given its name. It was moved to Rawnsley Colliery in May 1963, just two months after this photograph was taken, and then scrapped at Chasetown in December 1964.** ***Sunday 24th March 1963***

Topham **was also at West Cannock Colliery that day. It is a W.G. Bagnall of Stafford 17 x 24in. outside cylinder 0-6-0 saddle tank with the Works No. 2193. It had been supplied new to the West Cannock Colliery Co. Ltd in November 1922 and was named after one of the colliery's owning families. At the time it was the largest industrial locomotive built by Bagnall and it was the only one of its type. It had 3ft 9in. wheels. In 1970 it was transferred to Cannock Wood Colliery for a few months. When no longer required, in November 1972,** ***Topham*** **went to the Foxfield Light Railway. In 1987 it moved on to the North Downs Steam Railway at Dartford and, when that was closed, to the Spa Valley Railway in 1996.** ***Sunday 24th March 1963***

No. 4 was only nine years old when seen here at West Cannock Colliery. It is a Hunslet Engine Co. 18 x 26in. inside cylinder 0-6-0 saddle tank with the Works No. 3806 and it had been acquired new for Rawnsley Colliery in 1953 but moved on to Cannock Chase in the same year. It was then transferred to West Cannock Colliery during the winter of 1961-62. When no longer required there it was saved by the Dean Forest Railway Preservation Society in 1973 and delivered to their site at Parkend in 1976. It is now named ***Wilbert,*** after the Reverend Wilbert Awdry who wrote the ***Thomas the Tank Engine*** books. *Monday 11th June 1962*

The 71 year-old No. 3 ***Hanbury*** shunting wagons at West Cannock Colliery. It was a Peckett 'X' Type 16 x 22in. inside cylinder 0-6-0 saddle tank built in 1894 with the Works No. 567 which had been delivered new to the Coppice Colliery Ltd. ***Hanbury*** had at times worked at Walsall Wood, Chasetown, Littleton and Hilton Main collieries, but it returned to Coppice Colliery before moving to West Cannock Colliery. It was scrapped during the winter of 1969-70. *Thursday 22nd April 1965*

Peckett 'W7' Type 14 x 22in. outside cylinder 0-4-0 saddle tank No. 67 *NCB Pelaw*, with the Works No. 2093, catching the early morning sun at Ravensworth Ann Colliery at half past six. Destined for the Pelaw Main Collieries Ltd, it was delivered new to the National Coal Board just after nationalisation in 1947. It was then allocated to several sites on the Pelaw Main Railway. *Monday 18th July 1966*

Chapter 5

National Coal Board North and South

Ravensworth Ann Colliery near Gateshead

The ex-Pelaw Main Collieries Ltd Ravensworth Ann pit, also known as Team Colliery, in the Durham Coalfield was opened in 1930 in an area where there were already collieries served by the Pelaw Main Railway. One feature of the system was its rope hauled inclines, some of which originally used stationary steam (later replaced by electric) winding engines and others which were gravity-worked using the weight of full wagons descending to raise empty ones. The Ravensworth Ann Colliery was situated between the top of the Allerdene and the foot of the Starrs inclines and a locomotive was based there until 1968 to work the wagons between them. In 1959 this section of the Pelaw Main Railway had been connected to, and absorbed into, the Bowes Railway. Part of this railway at the nearby Springwell Colliery was similarly between two rope-hauled inclines which still exist as part of the Bowes Railway museum complex. The Ravensworth Ann Colliery site is now more famously that of Antony Gormley's steel sculpture the 'Angel of the North'.

Another view of No. 67 *NCB Pelaw* at work at Ravensworth Ann Colliery a little later on that day. When it was withdrawn from service it was sent to the Bowes Railway Springwell Workshops and cut up there in December 1968. *Monday 18th July 1966*

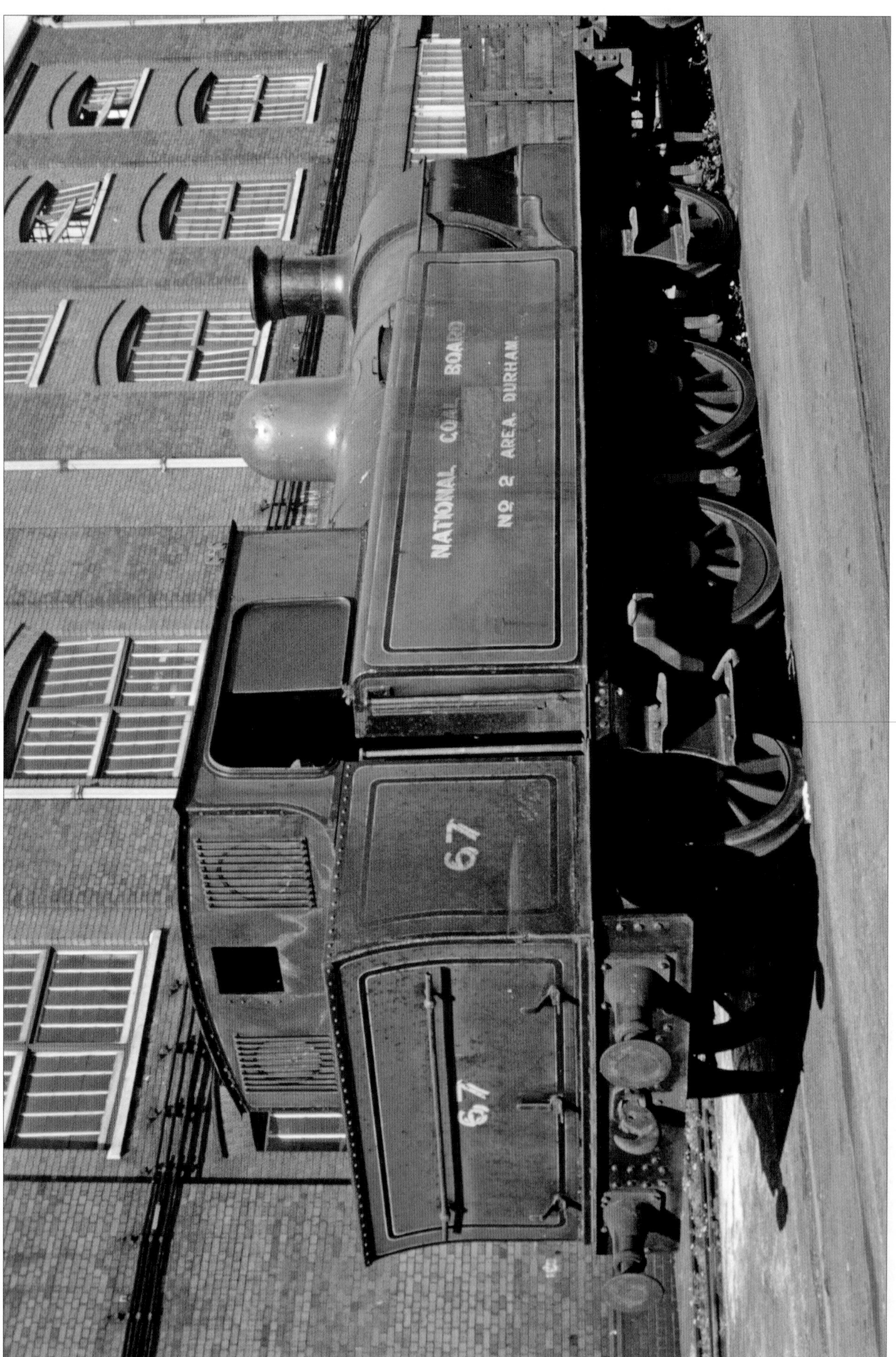

Ex-Taff Vale Railway '01' Class 17.5 x 26in. inside cylinder 0-6-2 side tank No. 28 was still in its National Coal Board identity No. 67 at Swindon Works. This Hurry Riches designed locomotive was built at West Yard Works, Cardiff, in 1897 as TVR No. 28. It became GWR No. 450 when the TVR was absorbed into it at the 1923 grouping but it was sold for military use at the Woolmer Instructional Military Railway at Longmoor three years later and became WD No. 205, and later WD No. 70205, and named ***Gordon.*** In 1947, two years after the end of the Second World War, the engine was sold for service at South Hetton Colliery in County Durham. It was withdrawn as NCB No. 67 in 1960 and donated to BR for preservation. It is now part of the National Collection and has been based at several sites, most recently on display at the Gwili Railway. *Sunday 20th September 1964*

Wearmouth Colliery

The ex-Wearmouth Coal Co. Ltd Wearmouth Colliery, earlier called Monkwearmouth Colliery, in Sunderland began production in 1835 and was the last deep mine in the once highly exploited Durham coalfield when it was closed in 1993. It is now the site of Sunderland Football Club's 'Stadium of Light' which opened in 1997 and is named after a miner's lamp. The exchange sidings were on the ex-North Eastern Railway near Monkwearmouth station.

No. 2B, a Hunslet 'Austerity' 18 x 26in. inside cylinder 0-6-0 saddle tank, was built in 1944 with the Works No. 3191 and it is seen here at Wearmouth Colliery. It had been delivered new to the Army Central Ammunitions Depot at Kineton in Warwickshire as WD No. 75140 and was transferred to Steventon Depot in Berkshire in 1945. In June 1947 it became No. 9 at Whitburn Colliery. It later worked at other collieries until it was transferred to Wearmouth already renumbered 2B in 1966. It had been fitted with a Giesl ejector in 1960 and nicknamed ***Funkenbanger***. It was scrapped in March 1969. *Monday 18th July 1966*

NCB locomotive ***Jean*** poses for a photograph with her Wearside 'Mackem' crew and other railway workers at Wearmouth Colliery, Sunderland. (A 'Mackem' is someone from the Sunderland area). This R. & W. Hawthorn, Leslie & Co. Ltd of Newcastle upon Tyne 17 x 26in. inside cylinder 0-6-0 side tank was built in 1909 with the Works No. 2769 and delivered new to the Wearmouth Colliery Co. Ltd. It had relatively large 4ft 1in. wheels. *Monday 18th July 1966*

Andrew Barclay 17 x 24in. inside cylinder 0-6-0 side tank locomotive *Will* was also at Wearmouth Colliery that day. It was built in 1909 with the Works No. 999 and delivered new to the Wearmouth Coal Co. Ltd. It was transferred to the nearby Hylton Colliery at the end of the year this photograph was taken and was scrapped in February 1968. *Monday 18th July 1966*

Robert Stephenson & Hawthorns Ltd 14 x 22in. outside cylinder 0-4-0 saddle tank No. 4 was also delivered new to the Wearmouth Coal Co. Ltd. It was built in 1938 with the Works No. 6945. Clearly already out of use for some time when seen here, it was scrapped in September 1966. *Monday 18th July 1966*

Jean, the Hawthorn, Leslie 0-6-0 side tank, was creating exceptional clouds of smoke at Wearmouth Colliery. ***Jean*** was scrapped in February 1971.
Monday 18th July 1966

Another locomotive with the No. 4 was at work at Wearmouth Colliery that day. It was also a Robert Stephenson & Hawthorns product but it was a larger 18 x 24in. outside cylinder 0-6-0 saddle tank built in 1951 with the Works No. 7690. It was transferred to Hylton Colliery five months later. It was scrapped in February 1968. British Railways 'Q6' Class 0-8-0 No. 63436 can be seen behind. *Monday 18th July 1966*

A clearer look at No. 63436 at Wearmouth Colliery. This Ravens designed 'Q6' Class 0-8-0 was built by Armstrong, Whitworth as North Eastern Railway No. 2279 in 1920. It was allocated to Sunderland shed (52G) at the time the photograph was taken. It was withdrawn in April 1967 and sold for scrap to Hughes Bolckow at North Blyth. *Monday 18th July 1966*

Seaham Colliery

The ex-Londonderry Collieries Ltd Seaham Colliery was connected to the ex-North Eastern Railway Sunderland to Hartlepool line by a short branch and directly to Seaham Harbour. The colliery closed in 1987 when workings were merged with Vane Tempest Colliery which closed in turn in 1994.

No. 38, a Robert Stephenson & Hawthorns 15 x 22in. outside cylinder 0-4-0 saddle tank built in 1953 with the Works No. 7756 is seen working hard at Seaham Colliery. Based on the Lambton Railway when new, it had been transferred to Seaham from the Lambton Railway Philadelphia sheds the previous year. The unusual shaped rounded cab roof was for access through the Lambton Railway Staithes tunnel. *Wednesday 20th July 1966*

Another look at No. 38 at work at Seaham Colliery. It was scrapped in September 1968. *Wednesday 20th July 1966*

Seaham Harbour Dock Co. Ltd

Although not actually part of the National Coal Board the Seaham Harbour Dock Co. Ltd system is included here since its main traffic was coal from the local collieries and it had originated as part of the Londonderry Railway. The third Marquis of Londonderry's colliery interests and Seaham Harbour were served by a network of railways first established in 1831. At the turn of the century the Londonderry Railway, which had become extensive in the area, was sold to the North Eastern Railway which operated the lines from October 1900 but the collieries remained the property of Londonderry Collieries Ltd and the Seaham Harbour Dock Company Ltd was formed to serve the docks. Steam operation continued until 1967 when those locomotives still in service, with the exception of a rare Lewin built example, were withdrawn and scrapped and a fleet of five new English Electric 0-6-0 diesel hydraulic locomotives was delivered. The port is now operated by the Victoria Group and still retains its rail connection.

No. 18 is a Stephen Lewin's Iron Foundry of Poole in Dorset 0-4-0 saddle tank which was built as a well tank with the Works No. 683, probably in 1877 although a number of earlier dates have been suggested. It was delivered new to the Marquis of Londonderry's Railway at Seaham Harbour where it is seen here, out of steam but still in service. It was twice rebuilt at the Seaham Harbour Works, first as a side tank and then, in 1936, as a saddle tank as seen in the photograph. It continued in use until around the end of 1969 apparently because it could run under the staiths on the quayside where the diesels could not operate. Fortunately it escaped the cutter's torch and found a new home at the North of England Open Air Museum at Beamish. It was first returned to its early appearance but is now to be seen fully restored to its later saddle tank form and in green livery. *Wednesday 20th July 1966*

Juno, a Hawthorn, Leslie 16 x 24in. outside cylinder 0-6-0 saddle tank built in 1922 with the Works No. 3527, was delivered new to the Seaham Harbour Dock Co. Ltd. It was scrapped early the following year. *Wednesday 20th July 1966*

Another locomotive at Seaham that day was No. 54, a Robert Stephenson & Hawthorns 16 x 24in. outside cylinder 0-4-0 saddle tank. It was built in 1947 with the Works No. 7346 and had come to Seaham in 1963 from Dorman Long, Britannia Works in Middlesbrough, where it had gained its large painted number. It was one of six large Robert Stephenson & Hawthorns locomotives which came from there and the Acklam works at Middlesborough at that time. It was scrapped five months after this photograph was taken. *Wednesday 20th July 1966*

Kilmersdon Colliery in Somerset

The colliery railway ran to the exchange sidings on the ex-Great Western Railway Frome to Radstock line which were reached via a gravity-worked rope-incline, also called a self-acting incline, which relied on the weight of full wagons to raise the empty ones. It was 160 yards long with an overall gradient of 1 in 4. Much of the coal was destined for Portishead Power Station. It was the last working colliery in the Somerset Coalfield when it closed in 1973. The railway trackbed is now part of the Colliers Way cycle route.

Peckett 1788 seen at work at Kilmersdon Colliery. This Peckett 'R3' Type 12 x 20in. outside cylinder 0-4-0 saddle tank was built in 1929, with the Works No. 1788, for the Writhlington Collieries Company, owners of Kilmersdon. The colliery closed in 1973 and the locomotive was preserved, first at the now closed Somerset and Dorset museum and then with the S&D collection at the West Somerset Railway Washford station where it was repainted in Somerset and Dorset blue livery and given the name ***Kilmersdon***. It was loaned for a time to the Helston Railway. *Thursday 3rd March 1966*

Another look at Peckett No. 1788 at work at Kilmersdon Colliery. Although it spent most of its working life at Kilmersdon it occasionally also worked at the nearby Norton Hill Colliery. The locomotive took full wagons to, and empty wagons from, the rope-hauled incline to the interchange sidings with British Railways. *Thursday 3rd March 1966*

The 160 yard long gravity balanced rope-hauled incline at Kilmersdon Colliery in operation. The interchange sidings and the British Railways Radstock to Frome line can be seen at the bottom. *Thursday 3rd March 1966*

Hunslet Engine Works No. 1684 was also at Kilmersdon Colliery the same day. This Hunslet 12 x 18in. outside cylinder 0-4-0 side tank was built in 1931. It was originally delivered to Hall's Coulsdon lime quarry at Redhill. At the end of its time at Kilmersdon, in 1968, it was bought for preservation first at the Bleadon and Uphill museum near Weston-super-Mare. In 2006 it was moved to the Middleton Railway and has been named the ***Mendip Collier.***
Thursday 3rd March 1966

Leicester Power Station No. 3 seen working hard. This Robert Stephenson and Hawthorns Ltd outside cylinder 0-4-0 saddle tank was built in 1950 with the Works No. 7680. It worked at Leicester alongside two Andrew Barclay fireless locomotives. After it was no longer required at the power station it went to the Fulstow steam centre in Lincolnshire and was given the name *Fulstow No. 1. Friday 3rd January 1964*

Nechells No. 1 was one of two Peckett 'W5' Type 14 x 20in. outside cylinder 0-4-0 saddle tanks in use at Nechells Generating Station in the first half of the 1960s and it was hard at work here. Built in 1916 with the Works No. 1438, it had been supplied new to the City of Birmingham Electric Company at Nechells. When No. 1 was no longer required it was transferred to Northampton Power Station as a standby locomotive in 1972 and three years later it was sold for scrap but fortunately it was then purchased for preservation, first at the East Anglian Railway Museum at Chappel & Wakes Colne station, Essex, and later at the Appleby Frodingham Railway Preservation Society at the Scunthorpe Steelworks in Lincolnshire. Note the 'Crossing No Gates' sign. This type of road sign was replaced by the ones we see today in the mid-1960s as a result of the Warboys Committee recommendations of 1963. *Saturday 10th April 1965*

Chapter 6

Midlands Power Production - Electricity and Gas

Central Electricity Generating Board, Leicester Electricity Generating Station

Leicester Freeman's Meadow Power Station in the East Midlands started operation in December 1922. Leicester City football club bought part of the site after it closed in 1972 and a new 32,500 seater stadium was opened there in July 2002 to replace the more than a century old Filbert Street ground. Formerly known as the Walkers Stadium, it is now known as the King Power Stadium after the duty free company which belonged to the club's Thai businessman owner, Vichai Raksriaksorn, who was killed in a helicopter crash outside the stadium in October 2018.

Central Electricity Generating Board, Nechells Generating Station, Birmingham

This ex-City of Birmingham Electric Supply Department generating station replaced an earlier temporary wartime power station and was opened by the Prince of Wales in June 1923. Because of this event it was unofficially called the Prince's Power Station. The larger Nechells B Power Station became operational in 1954. Several powerful 0-6-0 side tank locomotives with a tractive effort of 27,000lbs, higher than the ex-LM&SR Class '5' locomotives passing by on the main line, were employed to haul 1000 ton coal trains from the British Railways exchange sidings at Bromford Bridge, on the former Midland Railway Birmingham to Derby line, to the coal tipplers. Steam working finished when diesels took over towards the end of 1971 and rail traffic finally ended when the B power station closed in July 1982. It was demolished in 1988 and it is now the site of the Star City entertainment complex which was opened by George Clooney and Mark Wahlberg in July 2000.

BELOW: No. 2, the other Peckett 'W5' Type 14 x 20in. outside cylinder 0-4-0 saddle tank at Nechells, was also seen that day. It was built in 1917 with the Works No. 1478 and, like *Nechells No. 1*, it had been supplied new to the City of Birmingham Electric Supply Department Nechells Power Station. It was transferred to Hams Hall Power Station at the start of the 1950s but had been returned to Nechells by 1957. The locomotive was scrapped in the summer of 1972. *Saturday 10 April 1965*

No. 3 standing on a turntable at Nechells Power Station. Turntables were not usually found on industrial lines because they used tank engines. No. 3 was one of two Robert Stephenson & Hawthorns Ltd 18 x 24in. outside cylinder 0-6-0 side tank locomotives on site at the time. A third joined the following year. Built in 1949 (Works No. 7537), No. 3 was supplied new to the British Electricity Authority at Nechells. In 1972, the year after steam working finished, it went to the Battlefield Line of the Shackerstone Railway Society in Leicestershire where it was given the locally appropriate name ***Richard III. Saturday 10th April 1965***

No. 4, a Robert Stephenson & Hawthorns Ltd 18 x 24in. outside cylinder 0-6-0 side tank built to the same design as No. 3 in 1951 with the Works No. 7684 was at Nechells Power Station. It had at first been delivered to Meaford Power Station at Barlaston, near Stone in Staffordshire, as *MEA No. 2* but it was soon transferred to Nechells where it became their No. 4. Like No. 3, it was bought for preservation when redundant and it went to the Battlefield Line in June 1973. In 1996 it moved on to the Foxfield Railway at Blythe Bridge in Staffordshire where it was repainted in the original Meaford Power Station green livery with the number 2. The locomotive was moved again in 2010, this time to the Chasewater Railway in Staffordshire, where it became No. 4 once more. *Saturday 7th April 1962*

Central Electricity Generating Board, Hams Hall Power Station, Warwickshire

There were in fact three power stations at Hams Hall. The first station was opened in 1929, the second in 1942 and the third in the 1950s. In the 1960s all three were in full production. Like Nechells Power Station, Hams Hall had a number of the powerful Robert Stephenson & Hawthorns Ltd 0-6-0 side tank locomotives that were needed to deliver coal around the extensive rail system which served all three sites. There were as many as eight of these in the Hams Hall fleet at times and there were eventually 12 of the type in the West Midlands area. All three Hams Hall power stations have now been closed down and demolished. Today it is the site of the Hams Hall Distribution Park and, still with a rail theme, the Hams Hall Channel Tunnel Freight Terminal.

No. 13, an 18 x 24in. outside cylinder locomotive built by Robert Stephenson & Hawthorns Ltd in 1955 with the Works No. 7846, was in action still sporting the pre-1958 'Central Electricity Authority' on its tank sides. Delivered new to Hams Hall, No. 13 worked until 1972 when it was bought for preservation. In 1996, after spending time at various locations including the North Downs Steam Railway where it gained the name ***North Downs***, it arrived at the Spa Valley Railway at Tunbridge Wells in Kent where it worked the first passenger trains on the preserved line. It has since been sold to the Ferryhill Railway Heritage Trust in Aberdeen. *Sunday 8th April 1962*

Also that day, a partly repainted No. 5 was seen moving up to the tower to take on water. This 18 x 24in. outside cylinder 0-6-0 was built in 1936 and was the sole locomotive at Hams Hall built by Hawthorn, Leslie & Co. Ltd, Newcastle upon Tyne (Works No. 3904) before, in the following year, its locomotive building interests were transferred to Robert Stephenson & Co. which built the later engines of this type. For a short time, from October 1954 to August 1955, No. 5 had worked at Nechells. It was scrapped during the summer in 1968. *Sunday 8th April 1962*

I visited the site again the following year. This was just a few weeks after the end of one of the coldest winters on record, the 'Great Freeze' of 1963, so Hams Hall was exceptionally busy rebuilding the coal stocks. No. 8, a Robert Stephenson & Hawthorns Ltd 18 x 24in. outside cylinder 0-6-0 side tank built in 1942 with the Works No. 7067, was hard at work. It was transferred to Nechells Power Station in Birmingham in December 1966 and scrapped in 1972.
Sunday 24th March 1963

Taken the same day, some of Hams Hall's impressive array of cooling towers can be seen in the background behind No. 10. This was a Robert Stephenson & Hawthorns Ltd 18 x 24in. outside cylinder locomotive built in 1949 with the Works No. 7536 . It was scrapped during the summer of 1968.
Sunday 24th March 1963

No. 12, Robert Stephenson & Hawthorns Ltd 18 x 24in. outside cylinder 7845 of 1955, was also in action that day. It had been delivered new to Hams Hall. Like No. 13, it was still carrying the pre-1958 *Central Electricity Authority* on its tank sides. No. 12 can now be seen on static display at the Dales Countryside Museum at the old Hawes railway station in Yorkshire where it has been painted in British Railways lined black livery and given the BR number 67345 which originally belonged to a Great Eastern Railway 'G5' Class 0-4-4 side tank designed by Wilson Worsdell. The real No. 67345 used to work on the Wensleydale line from Hawes and trains may one day again run through the station if a Wensleydale Railway project to extend to Garsdale materialises. *Sunday 24th March 1963*

No. 7 was another Hams Hall Power Station Robert Stephenson & Hawthorns Ltd 18 x 24in. outside cylinder 0-6-0 side tank in action that day. It was built in 1938 with the Works No. 6965. It was scrapped during the summer of 1972. *Sunday 24th March 1963*

Breaking the monopoly of the 0-6-0 side tanks at Hams Hall, No. 4, a Peckett 'W6' Type 14 x 22in. outside cylinder 0-4-0 saddle tank built in 1928 (Works No. 1738) and supplied new to Hams Hall, seen here shunting the wagons. It was one of two similar Pecketts in use there at the time. By 1968 this locomotive had been sold to a Severn Valley Railway member and it went to Bridgnorth on that line. *Saturday 10th April 1965*

By the date of this photograph, No. 4 was in preservation and was on show at an open day for 'day members' that pre-dated the Severn Valley Light Railway Order, which was granted in November 1969. GWR 0-6-0 No. 3205 is seen just behind. LM&SR Ivatt designed, built by British Railways after nationalisation, 2-6-0s No. 43106 and No. 46443 were also in steam that day. This was at the end of the very month that saw the 11th August 'Fifteen Guinea Special', officially the last steam hauled British Railways main-line passenger train, and the introduction of the BR steam ban the following day. Later No. 4 was moved to the South Devon Railway and then to Titley Junction station in Herefordshire where it was given the identity of *No. 6 Percy* from the ***Thomas the Tank Engine*** books. *Saturday 31st August 1968*

West Midlands Gas Board, Windsor Street Gas Works, Birmingham

This ex-Birmingham Corporation gas works became part of the West Midlands Gas Board on nationalisation on 1st May 1949. It was connected by rail to the ex-London & North Western Railway Aston Branch which joined the main line near the ex-L&NWR locomotive shed at Aston. Rail traffic continued with diesel shunters until the gas works was closed in 1974.

I was able to photograph two of the, then, steam allocation of four at the West Midlands Gas Board Windsor Street Gas Works. Standing out of steam, *Alan* was a 14 x 22in. outside cylinder 0-4-0 saddle tank built by Andrew Barclay in 1938 with the Works No. 2060 and supplied new to the Birmingham Corporation Gas Department. It was withdrawn from service and sent to John Cashmore and Co. Ltd of Great Bridge for scrap in July 1966. ***Saturday 7th April 1962***

No. 3 was the locomotive on duty shunting at the Windsor Street Gas Works when seen here. It was a Peckett 'Greenhithe' Type 14 x 22in. outside cylinder 0-4-0 saddle tank built in 1944 with the Works No. 2058. With its distinctive low cab, it was known as *Greenhithe* but the name was only painted on the tanks underneath the number plates. Delivered new to the Birmingham Corporation Gas Department, it was one of three Pecketts at Windsor Street at the time and, with sister Peckett No. 4 *Windsor* (built in 1930), was one of last two steam locomotives in service until they were finally sent to John Cashmore and Co. Ltd of Great Bridge for scrap in March 1969. The fourth locomotive, No. 1 (built by Peckett in 1932) which was transferred to Coventry Gas Works in 1963 was also sent to Cashmore's and briefly reunited with the others in March 1969. ***Saturday 7th April 1962***

West Midlands Gas Board, Nechells East (Saltley) Gas Works

The Nechells East Gas Works had been called Saltley Gas Works until it was renamed in July 1963, just four months before this picture was taken. Rail connection was with the ex-Midland Railway Birmingham to Derby main line at Saltley. The gas works was closed in 1969.

West Midlands Gas Board No. 4, like No. 3 at Windsor Street, was a Peckett 'Greenhithe' Type 14 x 22in. outside cylinder 0-4-0 saddle tank. Delivered in 1945 with the Works No. 2070, it was working at Nechells East Gas Works in Birmingham when seen here. It was the only steam locomotive at this site at the time and shared work with a couple of diesel shunters. It went to John Cashmore and Co. Ltd, Great Bridge, for scrap in March 1968. *Sunday 3rd November 1963*

West Midlands Gas Board, Nechells (West) Gas Works

Conveniently close to Nechells East, situated on the opposite side of the Birmingham to Derby main line, was Nechells (West) Gas Works with an allocation of four steam locomotives. This gas works was connected to both the ex-Midland Railway Birmingham to Derby line at Duddeston Mill sidings and the ex-London & North Western Railway Birmingham to Walsall line near Vauxhall & Duddeston station. After steam locomotives were no longer in use two diesel shunters continued in service until the gas works was closed in 1969.

No. 8, an Andrew Barclay, Sons and Co. Ltd of Kilmarnock 16 x 24in. outside cylinder 0-4-0 saddle tank, in steam at Nechells (West) Gas Works. Built in 1932 with the Works No. 1992, and supplied new to Birmingham Corporation Gas Department, it was withdrawn from service and sent to Cashmore's at Great Bridge in December 1963 where it was cut up during the following month. This was one of two Barclays at Nechells at that time which worked alongside a Peckett and a Sentinel. *Saturday 7th April 1962*

Above: No. 10, a 4WTG vertical boiler Sentinel built in 1956 with the Works No. 9617, also in steam at Nechells (West) Gas Works. It had been supplied new to the Birmingham Corporation Gas Department in January 1957, just two years before the final Sentinel steam locomotives were constructed. No. 10 was an example of the more powerful 200 horsepower model of this type. There was also a 100 horsepower version. *Saturday 7th April 1962*

Right: The following year, just three weeks before the assassination of President J.F. Kennedy on 22nd November, No. 10 was on shed at Nechells (West) Gas Works. It was sent for scrap to Cashmore's at Great Bridge in March 1968. *Sunday 3rd November 1963*

Right: No. 11 was, and still is, a Peckett & Sons of Bristol 'OY' Type 16 x 24in. outside cylinder 0-4-0 saddle tank built in 1947 with the Works No. 2081 and delivered new to the Nechells Gas Works. Seen here at work at Nechells (West), it was a special short wheelbase version of the 'OY' Type because of the sharp curves at this site but apparently the unusually long overhang meant that it bucked considerably. It was relocated to the Swan Village Gas Works in West Bromwich in August 1965, where it joined a 180hp 0-4-0 diesel (North British Works No. 27544 of 1960) and performed there until the end of rail working in 1969. It was then bought privately for preservation and was moved to the Foxfield Light Railway at Blythe Bridge near Stoke on Trent in Staffordshire in August 1969. *Sunday 3rd November 1963*

West Midlands Gas Board, Soho Gas Works, Smethwick

The Borough of Smethwick Soho Gas Works, which, along with the other municipal gas works, became part of the West Midlands Gas Board on nationalisation on 1st May 1949, was connected to the London & North Western Railway main line from Birmingham to Wolverhampton. Rail traffic finished at the end of 1963.

LEFT: *Pinkney*, a Peckett and Sons of Bristol 'M5' Type 10 x 15in. outside cylinder 0-4-0 saddle tank, standing out of steam at Soho Gas Works. It was the only steam locomotive on site at the time, accompanied by a Ruston & Hornsby diesel shunter. *Pinkney* was built in 1934 with the Works No. 1836 and it was delivered new to the Borough of Smethwick works. It was named after Charles W. Pinkney who perfected a gas engine in 1889 and invented a Hydrocarbon Gas Producer and a Bituminous Coal Gas Generator. It was cut up at Soho in March 1964.
Saturday 7th April 1962

West Midlands Gas Board, Wolverhampton Gas Works

The Stafford Road Gas Works was built in 1849 and later enlarged. It continued in use until 1967 when natural gas from the North Sea replaced town gas. One part of the site is now the Wolverhampton Science Park and another part is an industrial estate.

No. 2 *Carbon*, a 14 x 20in. outside cylinder 0-4-0 Bagnall saddle tank, built in 1902 (Works No. 1673) and delivered new to the Wolverhampton Gas Company, at Wolverhampton Gas Works. It was rebuilt by Bagnalls in 1943. At the time there were two Bagnall and one Robert Stephenson and Hawthorns 0-4-0 saddle tank locomotives on site along with one diesel shunter.
Saturday 2nd November 1963

The other Bagnall locomotive at Wolverhampton was *Victory*, a newer 14 x 22in. outside cylinder 0-4-0 saddle tank built in 1942 with the Works No. 2661 and also delivered new to the Wolverhampton Gas Company. It is seen here out of steam. Both *Carbon* and *Victory* were scrapped in October 1965. *Saturday 2nd November 1963*

Abernant at work at Austin's Longbridge Works. Now preserved, it is a 13 x 20in. inside cylinder 0-6-0 saddle tank built in 1921 at the Boyne Works of Jack Lane, Leeds, to the specifications of Manning, Wardle. It had the Works No. 2015. *Abernant* had previously worked on the construction of the Cardiff Corporation Water Department Llwynon Reservoir at Cefn Coed in Brecknockshire and had moved to Longbridge in 1927 via the dealer Thomas Ward. *Saturday 11th May 1963*

Chapter 7

West Midlands Industry. Cars, Tyres, Paper, Cement and Chocolate

The British Motor Corporation Austin Motor Works in Longbridge

The Austin Motor Works rail link was with the ex-Great Western & Midland Joint branch from Halesowen to Longbridge. There was a station at Longbridge which was used solely by workmen's trains. The line closed in 1964 except for a short stub connecting the Longbridge Works with the ex-Midland Railway Birmingham to Gloucester main line. A Sentinel diesel hydraulic locomotive was tried in 1963 but it only stayed for four weeks leaving steam in sole charge until almost the end of the decade and the creation of British Leyland in 1968.

Other diesels started to arrive in 1969 but all the steam locomotives shown except *Abernant* survived at Longbridge into the next decade.

Austin 3, a Hunslet Engine Co. 14 x 20in. inside cylinder 0-6-0 saddle tank built in 1937 with the Works No. 1814, at the junction with the Longbridge to Halesowen branch. This was the year before the branch closed. *Austin 3* was scrapped in March 1971, three years after Austin had become part of British Leyland. *Saturday 11th May 1963*

Two years later, ***Austin II***, a Hunslet Engine Co. 14 x 20in. inside cylinder 0-6-0 saddle tank which was identical to ***Austin 3*** but built in 1936 with the Works No. 1692, was seen leaving the works heading towards the BR sidings. ***Austin II*** was delivered new after an unsuccessful trial with an Armstrong Whitworth 0-4-0 diesel-electric locomotive. It was scrapped at the end of 1970. *Saturday 10th April 1965*

No longer required in service at Longbridge, ***Abernant*** was sent to J. Cashmore's scrapyard at Great Bridge at the end of 1963 but fortunately it was not scrapped as it was presented for display in the Newdigate Street children's playground in Birmingham the following February. Seen here, it looked rather sad and neglected compared to the photograph taken at Longbridge only two years previously. In 1989 it was removed from the playground and placed at the Standard Gauge Steam Trust at Tyseley. It was moved again, first to the now closed North Woolwich Old Station Museum in 1992 and then to Peak Rail in 2002. Since 2003 it has been at the Great Central Railway (Nottingham) at Ruddington and has been given the number 5 and the name ***Arthur***. *Saturday 10th April 1965*

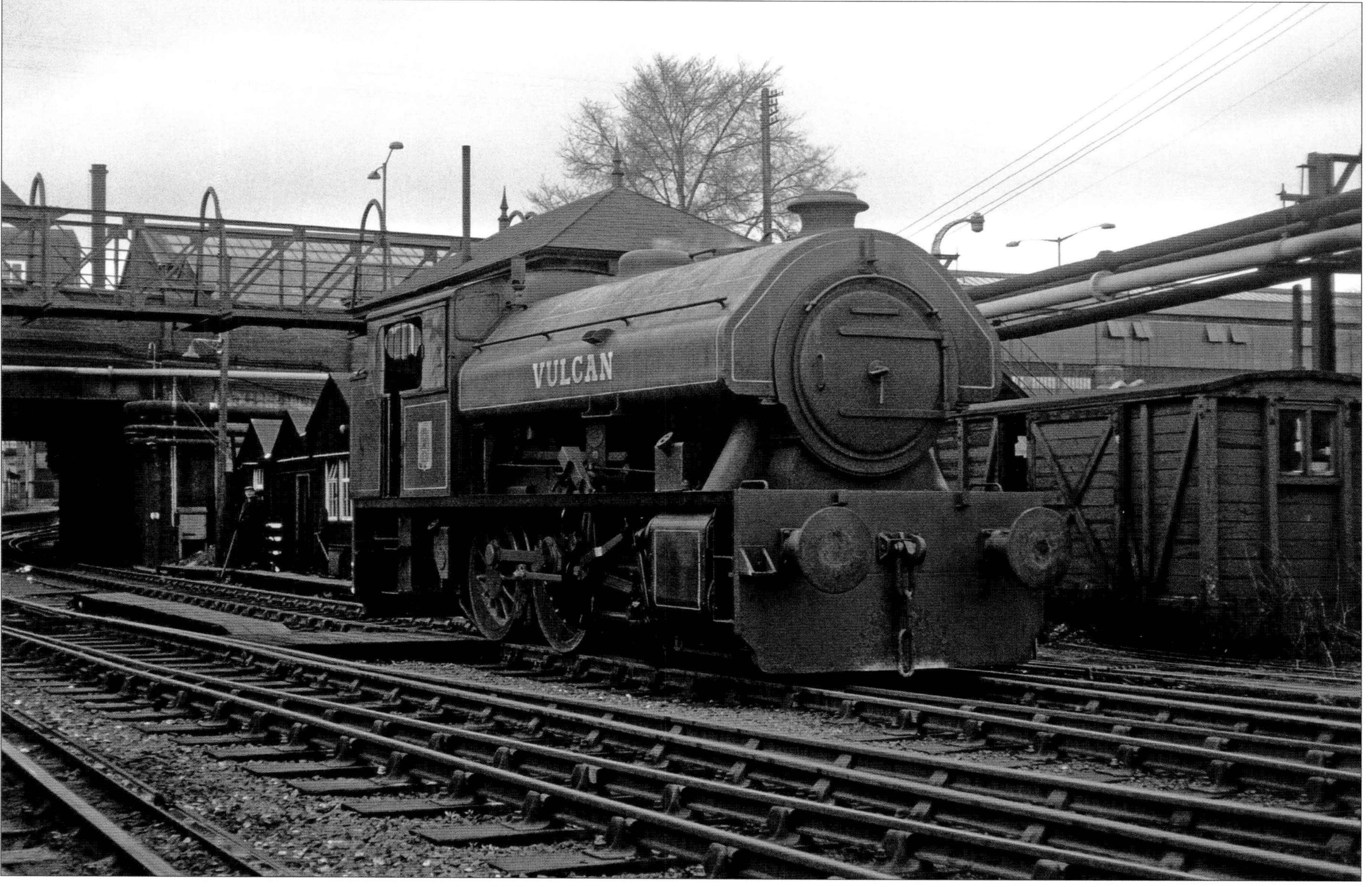

The impressive W.G. Bagnall 18 x 26in. outside cylinder 0-6-0 saddle tank *Vulcan* in action. Built in 1951, with the Works No. 2994, it was one of three powerful locomotives delivered to the Steel Company of Wales at Port Talbot and numbered 401, 402 and 403. When they were displaced by diesels in September 1957, 401 and 403 were bought by Austin's and named *Vulcan* and *Victor* . They had large 4ft 3in. wheels, Walschaerts valve gear, self-cleaning smokeboxes, rocking grates, and mechanical lubricators. Displaced yet again by diesels, *Vulcan* and *Victor* were both bought by the West Somerset Railway Company in 1973 and used during the early days of the line. *Vulcan* was later moved to the North Tyneside Railway Stephenson Railway Museum and renamed *Thomas Burt* after the trade unionist who became secretary of the Northumberland Miners' Association and a Liberal Member of Parliament. Its surviving sister, *Victor*, Works No. 2996, was out of steam in the shed on the day of my visit. It is now at the Lakeside & Haverthwaite Railway. The by then closed Halesowen Branch Longbridge station is just beyond the overbridge. *Saturday 10th April 1965*

Dunlop Rubber Company Ltd, Fort Dunlop

Cars need tyres and the best known British producer of these at the time was the Dunlop Rubber Company Ltd at the imposing Art Deco Fort Dunlop factory in Birmingham. I believe this factory was at one time the biggest in the world and it was, and still is in its new retail centre incarnation, a notable sight alongside the M6. Prior to the opening of the motorway in the 1970s this view was obviously not possible but the building was nevertheless very impressive. Steam working finished at the end of 1971 and an unusual standard gauge Motor Rail Ltd Simplex four wheeled diesel mechanical locomotive arrived in 1972. It was unusual because most of their products were narrow gauge. It continued to serve the site, which was connected to the ex-Midland Railway line between Bromford Bridge and Castle Bromwich, for around fifteen years until rail traffic ended.

On a wet Saturday No. 5, which did not carry its number, was in steam and shunting on the Fort Dunlop site. This 12 x 20in. outside cylinder Peckett 'R4' Type 0-4-0 saddle tank was built in 1943 (Works No. 2046) and was originally supplied to Morris Motors at Cowley, Oxford, from where it moved from cars to tyres at Fort Dunlop in November 1948. It was scrapped on site in September 1966 but Dunlop still used three steam locomotives. These were the Bagnall *Dunlop No. 6* and two Peckett 'W7' saddle tanks, both built in 1951, which came to Fort Dunlop from the Co-operative Wholesale Society's Irlam Soap Works in Lancashire in 1967 and 1966. All three have been preserved.
Saturday 10th April 1965

Less than a year after the end of steam on British Railways, *Dunlop No. 6*, still in industrial service, was on show at an early Standard Gauge Steam Trust open day at Tyseley, Birmingham, alongside the already preserved steam giants *Clun Castle, Kolhapur, Eric Treacy* and *Flying Scotsman*. Built in 1941 (Works No. 2648), *Dunlop No. 6* was one of a batch of nine 28-ton $14^1/_2$ x 22in. outside cylinder 0-4-0 saddle tanks built by W. G. Bagnall for the Ministry of Supply Royal Ordinance factories. It was rebuilt and converted from oil to coal firing and sold to Dunlop in 1965. After withdrawal in 1971 it spent some time at the Battlefield Line at Shackerstone in Leicestershire but since 2008 it is to be found on the Chasewater Railway in Staffordshire, where it was at first turned out in an NCB dark blue livery and the name *Linda*. It has since been repainted in green as *Dunlop No. 6* once again. *Sunday 4th May 1969*

Cadbury Brothers, Bournville

Visits to the Cadbury Brothers chocolate factory in the leafy Birmingham suburb of Bournville were understandably very popular. This was not necessarily to see its steam locomotives and I remember the gateman was taken aback when I only wanted to see the milk-chocolate liveried engines and not the chocolate making process. Despite this I was given one of the souvenir hinged metal chocolate boxes which, after I had eaten the contents, served me well as a pencil case for several years. After the Cadbury steam fleet was withdrawn, rail traffic at Bournville was left in the hands of four North British 0-4-0 diesel hydraulic locomotives which had been delivered in pairs in 1959 and 1961. The Cadbury rail system, which connected with the ex-Midland Railway line, operated until 1976.

There were four steam locomotives at Cadbury's Bournville factory when I visited. Two of them, both 0-4-0 side tanks which had been delivered new to Bournville, were out of steam inside the engine shed. No. 1 (left) was an Avonside 16 x 22in. outside cylinder locomotive built in 1925 (Works No. 1977) which when withdrawn from service in 1963 went to the Dowty Railway Preservation Society site at Ashchurch in Gloucestershire. No. 9 (right), particularly interesting because it had Walschaerts valve gear, was a 16 x 24in. outside cylinder Hunslet of Leeds product built in 1949 (Works No. 3665). It was scrapped on site in March 1966. *Monday 9th April 1962*

No. 6 was hard at work outside at Cadbury's on the same day. Looking smart in appropriate milk chocolate livery, it was an Avonside Engine Company 16 x 22in. outside cylinder 0-4-0 side tank built in 1923 with the Works No. 1921 and had been supplied new to Cadbury. It was sold to J. Round Ltd Metal Merchants of Wednesbury in January 1964 and scrapped there in 1967. *Monday 9th April 1962*

No. 10 was also at work that day. It was the last new steam locomotive to be purchased by Cadbury and one of the last Pecketts to be built. It was an 'OY2' Type 16 x 24in. outside cylinder 0-4-0 saddle tank built in 1955 with the Works No. 2156. It was sold to the National Coal Board in March 1963 and moved to Tilmanstone Colliery in Kent. It then spent a few months at Betteshanger Colliery and returned to Tilmanstone but in March 1964 it went to Chislet Colliery, also in Kent, where, in 1965, it was seen in an unusual silver livery which was, perhaps, an undercoat. It was cut up in August 1969. *Monday 9th April 1962*

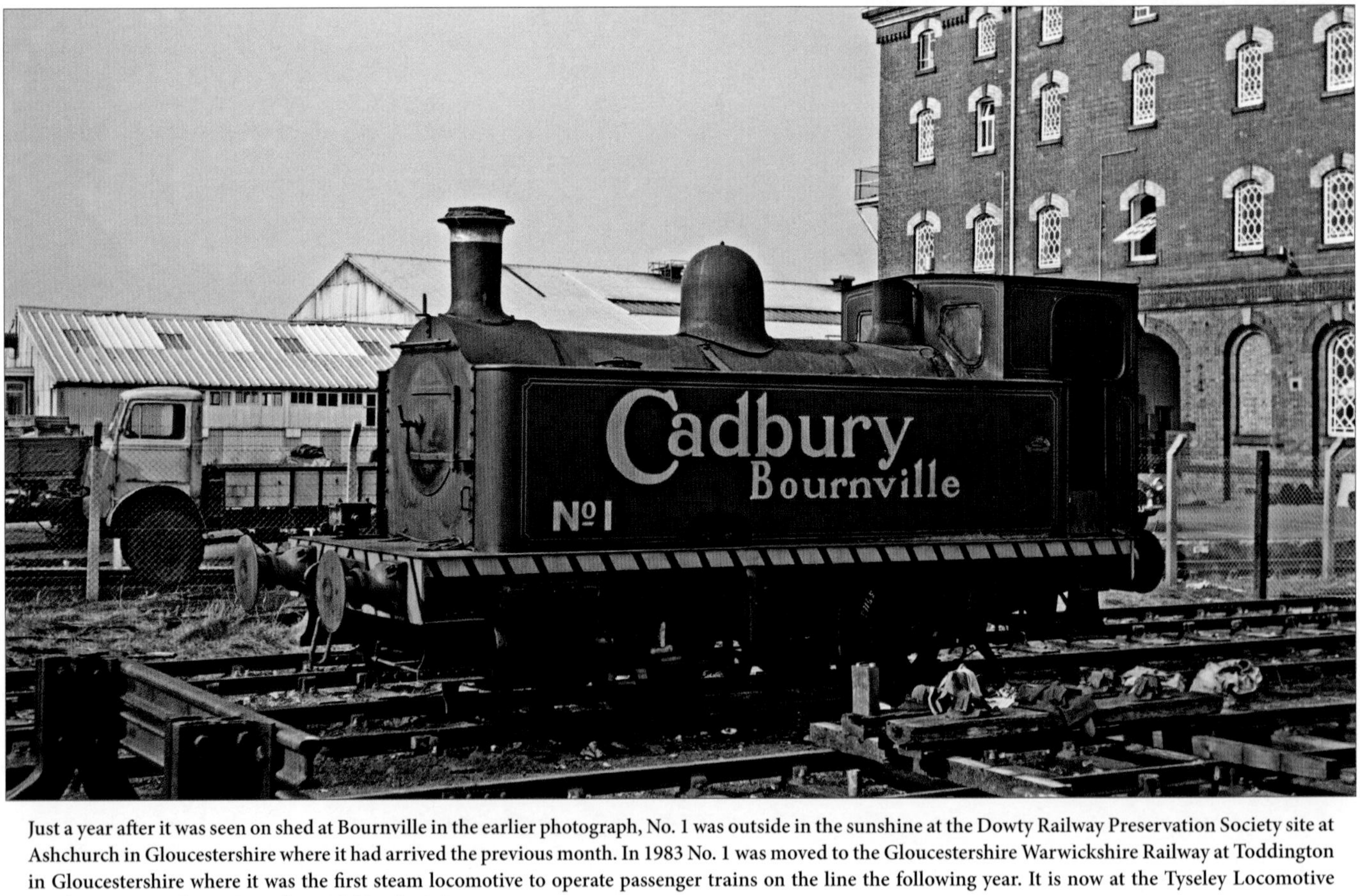

Just a year after it was seen on shed at Bournville in the earlier photograph, No. 1 was outside in the sunshine at the Dowty Railway Preservation Society site at Ashchurch in Gloucestershire where it had arrived the previous month. In 1983 No. 1 was moved to the Gloucestershire Warwickshire Railway at Toddington in Gloucestershire where it was the first steam locomotive to operate passenger trains on the line the following year. It is now at the Tyseley Locomotive Works in Birmingham. *Saturday 30th March 1963*

Alders (Tamworth) Ltd Paper Mill

One of the many smaller factories still using steam power in the 1960s was Alders Paper Mill at Tamworth in Staffordshire. It was of special interest because of the presence of ex-Great Western Railway No. 1340 *Trojan* which worked alongside a second, unnamed, locomotive. Alders railway line, which linked the paper mills with the London and North Western Railway Trent Valley Line at Coton Crossing, was closed in 1967. The paper mill was demolished at the end of the 20th century after about 200 years of production and housing now stands on the site.

Ex-Great Western Railway No. 1340 ***Trojan,*** a South Wales 0-4-0 saddle tank, wout of steam at Alders Paper Mill at Tamworth. This was just three days before the infamous Beeching report *The Reshaping of British Railways* was published. ***Trojan*** was built by the Avonside Engine Co. in 1897 (Works No. 1386) with 14 x 20in. outside cylinders and belonged to Messrs Dunn & Shute of Newport Town Dock until, in 1903, it was purchased by the Alexandra Docks Railway at Newport which was then absorbed into the GWR at the railway grouping in 1923. Sold to the Netherseal Colliery at Burton-on-Trent in July 1932, it was re-sold to Alders in 1947. Amazingly, it retained its GWR number plates. Now preserved in GWR livery, ***Trojan*** has been based at the Didcot Railway Centre since 1968. *Sunday 24th March 1963*

The second locomotive at Alders (Tamworth) Ltd is seen here out of steam. It was an Andrew Barclay 12 x 20in. outside cylinder 0-6-0 saddle tank built in 1918 with the Works No. 1576 but it did not carry a fleet number. Note the spark arrestor, surely an essential accessory for service in a paper mill. It had originally worked at Nobell's Explosives Co. Ltd at Pembrey in Caernarvonshire where the spark arrestor would have been even more necessary! The locomotive was bought from R.H. Neal of Park Royal, London, in 1927. It was scrapped on site in February 1968 four months after rail traffic had ceased. *Sunday 8th April 1962*

Rugby Portland Cement Works, New Bilton

There were several cement works with rail systems in what is usually considered to be the West Midlands but outside the more recently designated West Midlands Metropolitan County. In the middle of the 1960s the Rugby Portland Cement Works at New Bilton, near Rugby, was home to three steam locomotives. There was rail connection with the ex-London and North Western Railway Rugby to Leamington Spa line which closed to passengers on 13th June 1959 but the cement works was served until 1991.

No. 1, a 100hp 4WTG Sentinel of Shrewsbury built in 1953 with the Works No. 9559, in steam at New Bilton. It had arrived a year earlier from the company's Tottenhoe Quarries at Dunstable in Bedfordshire. In 1967 this locomotive went to Thomas Hill Ltd at Killamarsh in Yorkshire and a year later to the R.Y. Pickering & Co. Ltd Wagon Works at Wishaw in Lanarkshire. It continued in use there until the 1970s. It is now preserved on the Tanfield Railway, near Gateshead, Tyne and Wear, to where it was moved in 1979. *Wednesday 27th October 1965*

Fourteen weeks later, a Manning, Wardle 14 x 20in. inside cylinder 0-6-0 saddle tank was hard at work at New Bilton. Built in 1926 (Works No. 2047), it is notable because it was the last locomotive to be built by the Manning, Wardle Boyne Engine Works in Leeds which went into liquidation in 1927. It was ordered by Rugby Portland Cement in April 1926 and delivered in the August that year. *Wednesday 2nd February 1966*

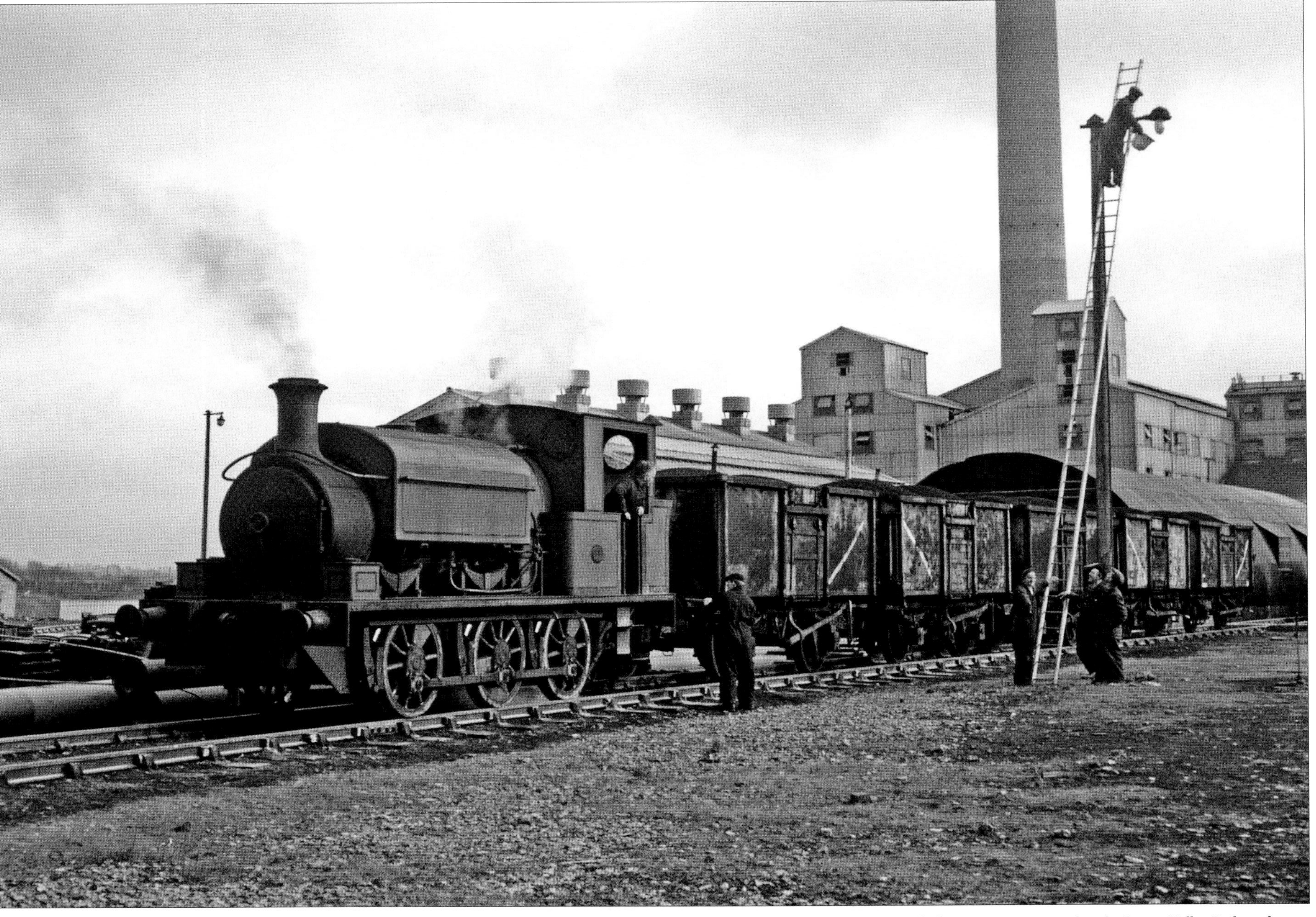

With the cement works at New Bilton in the background, No. 2047 is seen backing up its load of wagons. After it was withdrawn from service, the locomotive was moved to the Severn Valley Railway for preservation and named ***Warwickshire***. At first it was painted blue but it was later returned to a green livery. This picture poses the intriguing question: 'How many men does it take to change a light-bulb?'
Wednesday 2nd February 1966

Cunarder taking over a recently delivered train at the Harbury Cement Works exchange sidings. The Greaves Sidings signal box can be seen behind the locomotive. The sign on the right states 'British Transport Commission engines must not pass this notice'. *Cunarder*, a 14 x 20in. outside cylinder 0-6-0 saddle tank built as one of a batch of six by the Hunslet Engine Co. Ltd of Leeds (Works No. 1690) in 1931, has had an interesting history. It was supplied new to the consortium of John Mowlem & Son Ltd and Edmund Nuttal, Son & Co. (London) Ltd for use on the construction of the King George V dock at Southampton, which explains its name. In 1933 it was moved east for construction work on the Dover train ferry dock. In 1935 it was moved again to continue its seaside life at Wallasey on the sea wall and promenade contract there. During the Second World War it was used on several Royal Ordnance Factory construction contracts. After a number of post-war moves, *Cunarder* was sold and started work at Harbury in March 1957. *Tuesday 6th April 1965*

Associated Portland Cement Manufacturers Ltd, Harbury Cement Works

The Associated Portland Cement Manufacturers Ltd Harbury Cement Works exchange sidings were next to the ex-Great Western Railway Birmingham to Paddington main line opposite the Greaves Sidings signal box, named after the original owners of the works. In 1965 I finally discovered the identity of a locomotive that had caught my attention through the window of the train as I travelled from Paddington to Leamington Spa some years earlier. I had watched out on the left for the British Railways engine shed which I knew was just before Banbury station but there was a strange 'unidentified' saddle tank locomotive working in a siding on the left after the town between Fenny Compton and Leamington Spa. This was Harbury Cement Works and the locomotive must have been *Cunarder*.

British Railways No. 6697, a '5600' Class Charles Collett designed 0-6-2 tank engine built for the Great Western Railway by Armstrong Whitworth in 1928 (Works No. 985), seen delivering a rake of loaded wagons to the Associated Portland Cement Manufacturers Ltd Harbury Cement Works exchange sidings (Greaves Sidings) where the cement works shunter *Cunarder* was waiting. No. 6697 was the last of its class to be taken out of service and was bought by the Great Western Society in 1966, It is now at the Didcot Railway Centre. *Tuesday 6th April 1965*

Another look at *Cunarder* with the cement works behind. Fortunately, it still survives because in April 1969 it went to the Quainton Road Society in Buckinghamshire but its travels were not over. It has moved on to a number of other sites including the Swanage Railway, where it was rebuilt with side tanks, painted black and given the BR identity of scrapped Derby built LM&SR Fowler Dock Tank No. 47160. A more recent move was to a site near Poole for restoration as a saddle tank once again. Behind, on the right, is what I believe to be a Reliant Regal 'MkVI' three-wheeler. Its number plate, VBW 65, would have been issued in Oxfordshire in the spring or summer of 1962.

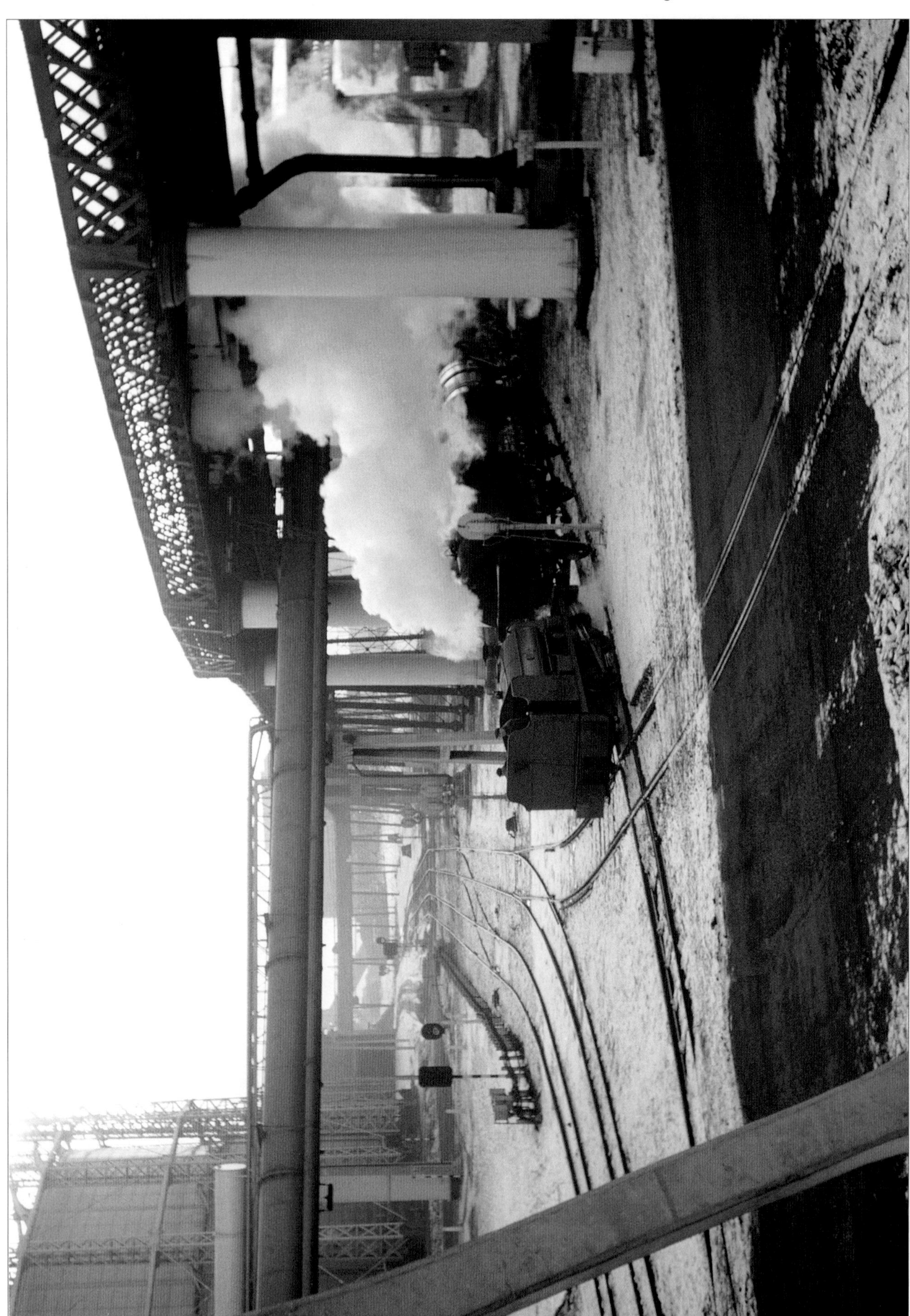

No. 9, an outside cylinder 0-4-0 saddle tank built by Peckett in 1920 with the Works No. 1574, was busily working at the North Thames Gas Board Beckton Products Works on a snowy December day in 1962. It had been delivered new to the Gas Light and Coke Co. at Beckton which was the predecessor of the North Thames Gas Board. It had dumb buffers and an open cab which would not have been ideal in that weather!

Chapter 8
The South of England

Beckton Gas Works and Beckton Products Works

The Gas Light & Coke Co. Beckton Gas Works, which had started production in 1870, came under the North Thames Gas Board on nationalisation in 1949. It was at one time the biggest in the world. The Products Works, dating from 1879, produced coal tar, ammonia and many other by-products of coal gas production. Gas manufacture ended in June 1969 and by-products the following year. The derelict site was used as the set for the city of Huế in the film *Full Metal Jacket*. The district of Beckton in East London is named after the gas works company founder, Simon Adams Beck. Gas works locomotives carried green livery and the Products ones were dark red.

Red liveried 0-4-0 fireless locomotive No. 12 was built by Hawthorn, Leslie in 1924 with the Works No. 3595 and is seen here at the North Thames Gas Board Beckton Products Works in December 1962. It is obvious that a locomotive without any fire had its advantages in a gas works although it had earlier been at work at the County of London Electric Supply Co. Ltd Barking Power Station.

Fireless locomotive No. 12 was at work again the following year at Beckton Products Works on a very wet day. *Tuesday 31st December 1963*

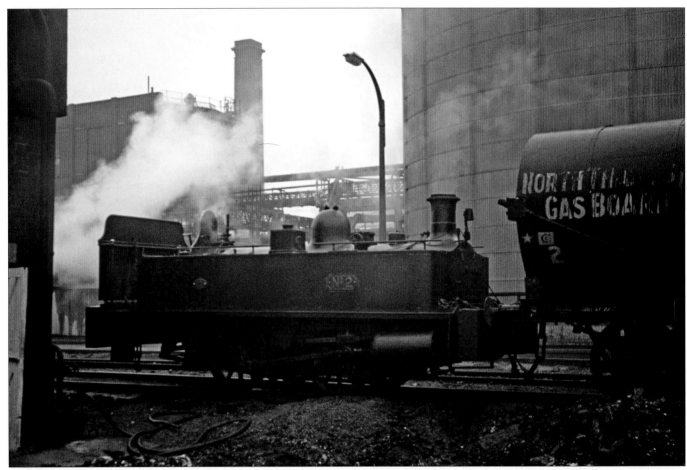

No. 2, an outside cylinder 0-4-0 side tank built by Neilson in 1892 and delivered new to Beckton, at work at the Products Works. It had the Works No. 4445. Sister locomotive No.1, Works No. 4444, is still in existence and was recently on sale at Preston Services near Canterbury. *Tuesday 31st December 1963*

No. 29 was an outside cylinder 0-4-0 side tank built by Neilson in 1897 with the Works No. 5231. It was hard at work at Beckton Products Works that day. It had been delivered new to Beckton Gas Works, hence its green livery, but was later transferred to the by-products works. It also had an open cab and dumb buffers. *Tuesday 31st December 1963*

No. 25 is a Neilson & Co. outside cylinder 0-4-0 saddle tank built in 1896 with the Works No. 5087 and it spent all its working life at Beckton Gas Works. It was obtained for preservation by the Industrial Locomotive Society and kept at Sheffield Park on the Bluebell Railway, where it is seen in this photograph, from 1961 until 1967 when it went on static display at the Bressingham Steam & Gardens Museum. A second preserved green Beckton Gas Works locomotive is at the Penrhyn Castle Museum in North Wales. It is No. 1, a Neilson & Co. 0-4-0 well tank built in 1870 with the Works No. 1561. *Sunday 21st April 1963*

United Glass Ltd, Charlton Works

At around the time of these photographs the United Glass Ltd Charlton works in Hope & Anchor Lane was the largest producer of glass containers in Europe. It had been the United Glass Bottle Manufactures Ltd works until 1950. Production ceased in 1966 and the site is now developed for warehousing including a major Sainsbury's depot. There were two very interesting steam locomotives at this site in the early 1960s accompanied by two diesel mechanical shunters; a four wheeled F. C. Hibberd Co. Ltd product with a Dorman 48hp engine and a more powerful 153hp Gardner engined Drewry Car Co. Ltd/Vulcan Foundry example.

This Edward Borrows & Sons Providence Works outside cylinder 0-4-0 well tank was built in 1906 with the Works No. 48 as a development of an 1866 design by James Cross. Named *The King*, it is seen here out of action at the United Glass Company Charlton Works. It had come to Charlton from the company's St. Helens Works in Lancashire in 1923. In September 1967 it went to the Kent and East Sussex Railway. It has since been at the Battlefield Line, Shackerstone, and is now based at the Ribble Steam Railway at Preston. *Wednesday 8th January 1964*

Of particular interest in action at the United Glass Charlton Works that day was ***Prince***, a 13 x 18in. outside cylinder 0-4-0 saddle tank designed by John Aspinall and built at the Lancashire & Yorkshire Railway's Horwich Works as L&YR No. 19 in 1910. At the railway grouping in 1923 it became LM&SR No. 11243. It was withdrawn from service in 1931 and sold to John Mowlem & Co. Ltd, a contractor, where it was given the name ***Bassett.*** It was then bought by the United Glass Bottle Company in 1933 and named ***Prince.*** ***Wednesday 8th January 1964***

Another look at ***Prince*** at the United Glass Charlton Works. It was sold to the Lancashire & Yorkshire Railway Preservation Society early in 1967 and it is now one of only two of the fifty-seven strong Horwich built L&YR Class '21', nicknamed 'pugs', to have survived into preservation. Like ***The King,*** it is now to be found at the Ribble Steam Railway at Preston. ***Wednesday 8th January 1964***

Central Electricity Generating Board, Bow Power Station

The Charing Cross and Strand Electricity Supply Corporation Ltd Bow Power Station in Marshgate Lane provided electricity to parts of the cities of London and Westminster. It became a constituent of the London Power Co. Ltd in 1925 and was nationalised, along with other power providers, in 1948. It closed in 1969.

No. 5, though not carrying the number, in steam at Bow Generating Station. It was a Hawthorn, Leslie outside cylinder 0-4-0 saddle tank built in 1927 with the Works No. 3653. It had previously worked at the Barking Generating Station until it was transferred to Bow in 1958. *Sunday 29th December 1963*

Met at Bow Generating Station. It is a Hawthorn, Leslie 10 x 15 in. outside cylinder 0-4-0 saddle tank built in 1909 with the Works No. 2800. It entered service with the Metropolitan Electric Power Supply Company at Acton, which explains its name, and was later transferred to Bow. Fortunately it has been preserved and it first went into store at the Kent and East Sussex Railway in 1967. After a number of moves, including to the Darlington North Road Station Museum and to Long Marston in Warwickshire, it was offered for sale in 2019, still in need of some restoration, by Penbryn Engineering near Caerphilly where it had resided for some time. *Sunday 29th December 1963*

Shipton-on-Cherwell Cement Works and Quarry

Usually considered to be in the South-East Region, Shipton-on-Cherwell Cement Works was constructed by the Oxford and Shipton Cement Company in the 1920s and taken over by Alpha Cement in 1934 which became part of Associated Portland Cement in 1938 and Blue Circle Industries in 1978. The cement works finally closed in 1986 and after it was abandoned there was an unsuccessful plan to develop an eco-town on the site. The quarry is now protected as a Site of Special Scientific Interest, important for wildlife and also for Jurassic fossils.

Alpha Cement Company No. 3, an Andrew Barclay outside cylinder 0-6-0 saddle tank with the Works No. 2041, was delivered new to Shipton-on-Cherwell in 1937 and is seen in action here. This cement quarry system was operated by what I believe were the last industrial steam locomotives in use in Oxfordshire, about four at this time, after two Peckett saddle tanks at Oxford gas works were withdrawn in 1961 and the demise of the large fleet at Oxfordshire Ironstone. I saw No. 3 again, withdrawn, in 1970. *Saturday 12th March 1966*

Associated Portland Cement Manufacturers Holborough Works, Snodland

The Holborough Cement Co. Ltd works at Snodland was established in 1923 and taken over by Associated Portland Cement Manufacturers, later known as Blue Circle Cement, in 1931. The Holborough works was closed in 1984 but there were later plans to extract chalk and clay from the quarry.

Hornpipe, a Peckett 'R2' Type 12 x 18in. outside cylinder 0-4-0 saddle tank built in 1928 with the Works No. 1756 and delivered new to the Holborough Cement Co. Ltd, at work at the Holborough Works. It was withdrawn from service in 1971 and went to the Quainton Railway Society site in Buckinghamshire in August the following year. Since 1987 it has been based at a private site in Berkshire but has been displayed elsewhere. *Monday 30th December 1963*

Longfield, a Peckett 'W6' Type 14 x 22in. outside cylinder 0-4-0 saddle tank built in 1928 (Works No. 1747) at the APCM Holborough Works at Snodland. It was delivered new to the British Portland Cement Manufactures Ltd Johnson's Branch Works at Greenhithe and transferred to Holborough in 1960. It was later loaned to the Crown and Quarry Cement Works at Frindsbury but when that site closed the year before this photograph was taken it returned to Snodland. In this photograph it has a cut down cab and chimney but these were later restored to the normal height. It was scrapped early in 1973. *Monday 30th December 1963*

This now preserved Aveling & Porter locomotive was also at the APCM Holborough Works at Snodland in Kent that day. It was a 2-2-0TG locomotive with the Works No. 9449 which was built at Rochester, in Kent, in 1926 and delivered new to the Holborough Cement Co. Ltd. It was clearly out of action as it had been withdrawn the previous year. *Monday 30th December 1963*

Another look at Aveling & Porter No. 9449 at the APCM Holborough Works at Snodland. The locomotive frames behind were probably the last remains of a scrapped Manning, Wardle 0-4-0 saddle tank called *Felspar*. *Monday 30th December 1963*

Aveling & Porter Works No. 9449 was given the name ***The Blue Circle*** and presented to the Bluebell Railway in 1964 but it was clearly not suitable for Bluebell passenger services and so it was transferred, first to the Northamptonshire Ironstone Railway Trust and then to the Buckinghamshire Railway Centre at Quainton Road in 1997. After further moves, to the Chinnor & Princes Risborough Railway and the Battlefield Line at Shackerstone, it went to the Rushden, Higham & Wellingborough Railway in 2015. It has visited several other sites including, more recently, the Nene Valley Railway, and it was hoped it would be present at the re-opening of the Leiston Works Railway in 2019, but unfortunately this was not possible. It is seen here at Sheffield Park on the Bluebell Railway. *Sunday 26th November 1967*

Another preserved Aveling & Porter locomotive resembling a traction engine on rails is the 0-4-0 geared well tank ***Sirapite*** which was built in 1906 with the Works No. 6158. It is seen here at a rally at Washington New Town in County Durham (Tyne and Wear since 1974), but ***Sirapite*** had first worked at Gypsum Mines Ltd at Mountfield in Sussex. This is where it obtained its name after a type of plaster made there. The story goes that the company planned to call the plaster 'Parisite', after plaster of Paris, but then realised that this was not really a suitable name and so changed it. In 1929 the locomotive was bought by Richard Garrett & Sons at Leiston for use between their works and the railway station. It was replaced by a battery electric locomotive in 1962 and was bought by Sir William MacAlpine. Some years later it was at a site in Kent until in 2004 the Trustees of the Long Shop Museum took it back home to Leiston where the factory railway was being restored. A Heritage Lottery Fund grant of £50,000 enabled work to return the locomotive to working order. It has recently visited the Mid Suffolk Railway. *Sunday 9th July 1967*

Howard Farrow Ltd, Colindale Plant Depot, Hendon

Trym had already been out of use for many years at Howard Farrow Ltd at Colindale when seen here. It is a Hunslet Engine Company 10 x 15in. outside cylinder 0-4-0 saddle tank built in 1883 (Works No. 287) which first went to the Cardigan Ironstone Company (later Stewarts & Lloyds), Corby, where it was named *Vigilant.* In 1903 it was sold on to Whitaker Brothers, contractor, in the Yorkshire West Riding, and soon after sold again to another contractor; Harold Arnold & Son of Doncaster. In 1920, after the locomotive was rebuilt, it moved on again, this time to Nott Brodie & Company of Northampton and used on a contract in Liverpool. It seems it was renamed *Trym* soon afterwards when it was was used in the construction of the Bristol Portway Road along the Avon Gorge which crosses the River Trym on a viaduct. It was later owned by Sir Robert McAlpine & Sons Ltd and then Howard Farrow Ltd at Colindale, Hendon. It gained a new boiler in 1942 but does not appear to have worked much longer. *Saturday 6th July 1963*

After years of disuse *Trym* was bought by a Quainton Railway Society member and moved to the Quainton Road site where it is seen in this photograph, without its cab but with some obvious restoration in progress. In November 1989 it went to the Northamptonshire Ironstone Railway Trust where it regained its name *Vigilant.* It is now at the Rutland Railway 'Rocks by Rail' Museum at Cottesmore. *Monday 1st September 1969*

Bowaters Pulp & Paper Mills, Sittingbourne

Established in 1863, Edward Lloyd Ltd Sittingbourne Paper Mill in Kent became part of the Bowater group as Bowater-Lloyd in 1948. The company later became Bowater's United Kingdom Pulp & Paper Mills Ltd. It was probably better known by enthusiasts for its 2ft 6in. gauge line between the paper mills at Sittingbourne and Kemsley Down and on to Ridham Dock on the Swale Estuary (see chapter 9) but there was also a standard gauge line which was connected to the Sheerness branch near Swale operated with two, now preserved, steam locomotives. These were replaced by two ex-British Railways '04' Class diesel-mechanical shunters. Interestingly, ex-London & South Western Railway William Adams designed '0415' Class 4-4-2 radial tank No. 488, now preserved on the Bluebell Railway, was acquired by the Ministry of Munitions in 1917, during the First World War, and used at Ridham Dock. The docks are still open but the railway has fallen out of use.

The ex-South Eastern & Chatham Railway 'P' Class 12 x 18in. inside cylinder 0-6-0 side tank *Pioneer II* was one of two standard gauge locomotives at Bowaters Pulp & Paper Mills Sittingbourne Works Ridham Dock site when seen here. It was built as No. 178 at Ashford Works in 1910 and it became Southern Railway No. 1178 at the grouping in 1923 and British Railways No. 31178 when the railways were nationalised. It was, at times, hired to Bowater's and when withdrawn by BR in 1958 it was sold to the company for use on the internal standard gauge branch to Ridham Dock where it worked until it was taken out of service with cylinder damage in 1969. It was then acquired by the Bluebell Railway and later sold to Southern Locomotives Ltd. In 2006 it was bought back by the Bluebell Railway where it is based today. *Monday 30th December 1963*

The second standard gauge locomotive at Bowaters Ridham Dock that day was *Jubilee*, a 12 x 18in. outside cylinder 0-4-0 saddle tank built in 1936 by W.G. Bagnall of Stafford (Works No. 2542) and delivered new to Edward Lloyd Ltd. It is now preserved at the East Anglian Railway Museum at Chappel & Wakes Colne. *Monday 30th December 1963*

James Hodson & Sons Flour Mill, Robertsbridge

'P' Class 12 x 18in. inside cylinder 0-6-0 side tank *Pride of Sussex* was out of steam at James Hodson & Sons flour mill at Robertsbridge. It was built at the South Eastern and Chatham Railway Ashford Works in 1908 and entered service early the following year with the number 753 but it was requisitioned during the First World War by the Railway Operating Division (ROD) in 1915. It later became Southern Railway No. 556 and British Railways No. 31556 and was sold to Hodson's when it was withdrawn from BR service in April 1961. When no longer required at the flour mill, in 1970, it was bought by the Kent & East Sussex Railway where, coincidentally, it had previously worked on hire from the Southern Railway for three short periods before and after the war. It became K&ESR No. 11.
Tuesday 20th September 1966

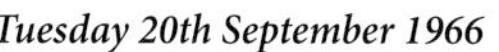

Corralls Coal Merchants, Southampton

Ex-London and South Western Railway Adams designed 'B4' Class outside cylinder 0-4-0 side tank No. 30096 working in Southampton Docks. It was built at the L&SWR Nine Elms Works in 1893 as No. 96 and it was named *Normandy.* It had spent its early life as a Southampton Dock shunter until displaced in 1947. Its final BR work was on shunting duty at Winchester goods yard but it was withdrawn in October 1963 and sold to Corralls coal merchants in Southampton. Seen here at Dibles Wharf, and still looking very much like a British Railways locomotive, it was used to move coal between Northam Yard and Dibles Wharf. It was later painted green and named *Corrall Queen.* In 1972 it was sold for preservation and it is now to be found on the Bluebell Railway where it was first steamed in 1986. *Thursday 9th April 1964*

Peckett Works No. 2128 was an 'R4' Type 12 x 20in. outside cylinder 0-4-0 saddle tank built in 1951 and delivered new to Southern Wharves Ltd the following year. It was at work at Dibles Wharf, Southampton here. *Thursday 9th April 1964*

Cheltenham Gloucester Road Gas Works

The ex-Cheltenham Gas Light and Coke Company Ltd Cheltenham Gas Works dated from 1829 and was sited between Gloucester Road and Tewkesbury Road next to the now closed Great Western Railway line between Cheltenham Malvern Road station and Stratford-upon-Avon (part of which is now the Gloucestershire Warwickshire Railway). It became the Cheltenham & District Gas Co. in 1931 and closed in 1969 but the impressive, mainly Gothic revival, Grade II listed administrative buildings and clock tower, now called Victoria House, is in use as offices for several private companies.

Peckett Works No. 1835 rests out of steam at the South Western Gas Board's Gloucester Road Gas Works in Cheltenham. This unnamed outside-cylinder 0-4-0 saddle tank was built in 1934 and delivered new to the Cheltenham & District Gas Company. *Monday 13th August 1962*

In the Scrapyard

After spending all its working life at the Royal Arsenal at Woolwich, ***Sturdee***, a Peckett 'E' Type 15 x 21in. outside cylinder 0-4-0 saddle tank built in 1940 with the Works No. 1986, awaiting the cutter's torch in the John Cashmore and Co. Ltd of Great Bridge scrapyard with three fellow Royal Arsenal Woolwich (ROF No. 1) locomotives. Two were 'W7' Type Pecketts called ***Byng*** and ***Horne***, and the third was ***Leviathan***, a Hawthorn, Leslie saddle tank. Sir Frederick Charles Doveton Sturdee was a noted Vice-Admiral and Admiral during the First World War who became Admiral of the Fleet in 1921. Many industrial locomotives were cut up by Cashmore's at Great Bridge as well as a large number of ex-BR locomotives. By strange coincidence, LM&SR Stanier designed 'Jubilee' 4-6-0 No. 45647 ***Sturdee,*** built at Crewe in 1935 and withdrawn in April 1967, was also scrapped at Cashmore's. *Saturday 7th April 1962*

Not from the South but included here as a second munitions locomotive awaiting scrapping, ***Risley Med Yard No. 109*** at the St. James Works yard next to Brackley station. This 1941 built Hudswell, Clarke outside cylinder 0-4-0 saddle tank, Works No. 1726, had arrived in 1961 from the Royal Ordnance Factory at Risley near Warrington. After its wartime munitions role, Risley became the site chosen for nuclear weapon development and, a little later, for United Kingdom Atomic Energy Authority civil nuclear research. Because of the sensitive nature of the site it is unlikely that there are many photographs of this locomotive in action there. This contractor's yard had been owned by E.L. Pitt & Co. (Coventry) Ltd until the previous month when it became R. Fenwick & Co. Ltd. *Tuesday 6th April 1965*

Industrial Preservation

Swanscombe on display at Quainton Road. It is an 11 x 18in. outside cylinder 0-4-0 saddle tank built by Andrew Barclay with the Works No. 699 which was delivered new to the Northfleet Coal & Ballast Co. Ltd in Kent in 1891. It was transferred to the company's West Thurrock Wharf in 1912 which was taken over by the Thurrock Chalk and Whiting Company. It was bought for preservation by a Quainton Railway Society member in 1965 and after a period in store arrived at Quainton Road just over four months before this photograph was taken. It is, apparently, the oldest Barclay locomotive in preservation in the United Kingdom.
Monday 1st September 1969

Andrew Barclay 10 x 18in. outside cylinder 0-4-0 saddle tank 1398, built in 1915, on parade at the Longmoor Military Railway open day. It had worked at the Royal Naval Airship Station near Rochester in Kent where it was given the name ***Lord Fisher*** after an the naval reformer Admiral. It was soon transferred to the Air Ministry at Kingsnorth, Kent, and later to the Air Ministry Farnborough site. In 1942 it moved again, to the Blackwater Gas Works at Camberley, and yet again, in 1956, to the Southern Gas Board Hilsea Gas Works in Portsmouth where it was renamed ***T. Carmichael.*** When no longer required, it was bought by the Chapel Tramway in Southampton in 1961 to replace a Peckett for use at the docks. That line closed in 1967 and the locomotive was bought for preservation and moved to the Longmoor Military Railway. A proposed scheme to preserve part of the military railway did not materialise and the locomotive then went to the Somerset & Dorset Railway Heritage Trust at Radstock. This scheme was also unsuccessful and so in 1973 the locomotive was moved yet again, this time to the East Somerset Railway. It is now at the Yeovil Railway Centre. *Saturday 8th June 1968*

The small outside cylinder 8 x 12in. 0-4-0 side tank No. 12 *Marcia* at Rolvenden on the Kent & East Sussex Railway. It was built by Peckett in 1923 with the Works No. 1631 and it started in service at Constable's Matlock Quarries but was sold to Marcus Bain Ballochmyle Quarry at Mauchline in Ayrshire about ten years later. In 1943 it passed on to the Manchester Oxide Company at Pendleton via the West of Scotland Shipbreaking Co. at Troon. The company was taken over by Hardman & Holden Ltd of Agecroft in Lancashire and *Marcia* was named after the works Managing Director's wife. It was donated to the K&ESR in 1962 and sold to a member. It has run in steam there at times. *Tuesday 20th September 1966*

Gervase, a Sentinel vertical boiler 0-4-0 tank engine, was also at Rolvenden on the Kent & East Sussex Railway that day. It is a rebuild of a Manning, Wardle 0-4-0 saddle tank (Works No. 1472) originally delivered to J.S. Peters Merstham Grey Stone Lime Works near Croydon in 1900. It was rebuilt by Sentinel in 1928. In 1949 it was sold to the Standard Brick Sand Company at Redhill. It moved to the K&ESR in 1962 and was steamed but it was sold to Resco Railways Ltd in 1979. After remaining at the K&ESR gradually deteriorating for a number of years, *Gervase* was transferred to the Elsecar Heritage Railway near Barnsley in 2008 where restoration work began in earnest. It then went to Locomotive Maintenance Services based at the Great Central Railway (GCR) in September 2012 for completion of the work. It is now based at the Elsecar Heritage Railway. In 2021 it was sent to J.M. Steam Engineering Ltd at Quainton Road for overhaul. *Tuesday 20th September 1966*

No. 15 ***Hastings*** at Tenterden. It is a 13 x 18in. inside cylinder 0-6-0 saddle tank built by Hunslet Engine Company in 1888 with the Works No. 469 for the Manchester Ship Canal contractor T.A. Walker where it was named ***Liverpool***. Ten years later it was sold to another contractor, Price, Wills & Reeves, and was renamed ***Hastings*** and used in the construction of the Bexhill West railway branch line. After work on a contract at Immingham Docks it was sold again, this time to the Park Gate Iron & Steel Company in 1915. It was used at the Rotherham works until, in 1935, it was moved to Sproxton Quarry in Leicestershire. Rail haulage ended there in 1963 and the Kent & East Sussex Locomotive Trust were able to buy ***Hastings***, which had already been out of use for several years, for £250 along with a Manning Wardle saddle tank called ***Cherwell*** for £280. It was later resold to a private owner and then sold again and moved to the Mangapps Farm Railway Museum in 2002. In 2017 it was acquired by a member of the Elsecar Heritage Railway where it joined ***Gervase*** in March 2018. Restoration work was undertaken at the Weybourne workshop of the North Norfolk Railway and at Elscar. It steamed for the first time at Statfold Barn in May 2021 and first hauled passenger trains on the Chasewater Railway in the September. *Tuesday 20th September 1966*

Chapter 9

Industrial Narrow Gauge Miscellany

There were several interesting pockets of narrow gauge industrial steam still working in Britain in the 1960s. Two of these were at ironstone quarries in Northamptonshire: the metre gauge Stewarts & Lloyds Minerals Ltd Wellingborough (Finedon) quarries and the three foot gauge Kettering Ironstone Quarries systems. Another was the Bowater's United Kingdom Pulp & Paper Mills Ltd 2ft 6in. gauge railway at Sittingbourne in Kent.

Wellingborough Ironstone Quarries

The Wellingborough Ironstone Quarry metre gauge line was built by the Wellingborough Iron Company Ltd to convey ore from the quarries to the ex-Midland Railway Bedford to Leicester line and Wellingborough Iron Works. When the works closed on 29th October 1962 three Peckett locomotives continued to work in what were by then the Stewarts & Lloyds Minerals Ltd quarries until they in turn were closed, the last one in 1966, and it became the last of the narrow gauge ironstone quarry systems to pass into history. No's 85 and 86 were Peckett 'M7' Type locomotives. No. 87, a Peckett 'Special R4' Type, was added to the team in 1942. All three Wellingborough metre gauge Pecketts have survived into preservation. Peckett 'M7' No. 85 first went to the Bressingham Steam Museum before moving on to the Yorkshire Dales Railway at Embsay. No. 86 went to a plant contractor at Kettering and No. 87 to a contractor at Finedon. They were later reunited at the Northamptonshire Ironstone Railway Trust and they are now to be found near to home at the Irchester Narrow Gauge Railway Trust, Irchester Country Park, Wellingborough.

A 3ft 3in. (metre) gauge Peckett 'M7' Type 10 x 18in. outside cylinder 0-6-0 saddle tank, built in 1934 with the Works No. 1870, in steam and working at Wellingborough Quarries which had recently been taken over by Stewarts & Lloyds Minerals Ltd. This was one of a pair of locomotives delivered new to the Wellingborough Iron Company Ltd in September 1934 to work in the quarries. It would later become No. 85. *Tuesday 6th November 1962*

The future No. 85 seen resting for a while at the engine shed at Stewarts & Lloyds Minerals Ltd Wellingborough Quarries. Everyone was undoubtedly relieved to see such normality as it was just one week after the end of the Cuban Missile Crisis! *Tuesday 6th November 1962*

On the same day, an ex-London Midland & Scottish Railway Stanier '8F' Class 2-8-0 was seen crossing over the quarry branch tunnel on the ex-Midland Railway Wellingborough to Kettering line with Peckett 1870 (No. 85) below. Wellingborough Iron Works, which had closed just a week earlier, on 29th October 1962, can be seen on the other side of the line. The brick engine shed is prominent in the foreground. *Tuesday 6th November 1962*

The metre gauge Wellingborough Quarries system was still in operation when this photograph was taken despite the demolition of the ironworks. No. 85's twin, No. 86, was, of course, also a Peckett 'M7' Type outside cylinder 0-6-0 saddle tank built in 1934. It had the Works No. 1871. It had become No. 86, and the livery changed from black to green, in 1964. Note the spark arrester. *Thursday 24th February 1966*

On the same day No. 86 waited patiently as skips were craned onto four-wheel wagon frames. These wagons were built by G.&R. Turner at Langley Mill in Derbyshire and the frames carried two skips each. They had buck-eye couplings. The quarry system was closed eight months later, on 14th October 1966.

Kettering Ironstone Quarries

The Kettering Iron & Coal Co. Ltd extensive three foot gauge line ran from the quarries to the ex-Midland Railway Kettering to Leicester line north of Kettering where three blast furnaces were built. These were nationalised in 1951 and then bought by Stewarts & Lloyds Ltd five years later. The ironworks stopped production in April 1959 but quarrying continued for a few more years to supply Corby Ironworks. These photographs were taken during what were truly the last days of this system as quarrying, which began in 1870, had ceased on 24th October 1962, just thirteen days before they were taken.

Kettering Furnaces No. 7 was one of three handsome 3ft 0in. gauge 11½ x 17in. outside cylinder 0-6-0 saddle tanks supplied new to the Kettering Iron & Coal Co. Ltd by Manning Wardle. It was built in 1897 with the Works No. 1370 and is seen here in steam at, what was by then, Stewarts & Lloyds Ltd Kettering Ironstone Quarries. It had been rebuilt by Robert Stephenson & Hawthorns in 1950 and, sadly, was scrapped on site in June 1963. *Tuesday 6th November 1962*

Kettering Furnaces No. 7 doing a little light shunting. Presumably the locomotive was employed on some final tidying up duties since quarrying had ended. *Tuesday 6th November 1962*

Another view of *Kettering Furnaces No. 7.* Sister locomotive *Kettering Furnaces No. 8* has been preserved and, after display in the open in Kettering, was reported to be under restoration by the Welland Valley Vintage Traction Club at Market Harborough. *Tuesday 6th November 1962*

Bowater's Railway

Probably the best known narrow gauge industrial system operating in England at the time was the 2ft 6in. gauge Bowater's United Kingdom Pulp & Paper Mills Ltd operation at Sittingbourne in Kent. The line connected the paper mills at Sittingbourne and Kemsley Down to Ridham Dock on the Swale Estuary where logs and wood pulp arrived and paper left by ship. In the early 1960s there were thirteen narrow gauge steam locomotives, two of which were fireless, based there plus one English Electric battery electric and one Hunslet diesel locomotive. There was also a standard gauge line which was connected to the Sheerness branch near Swale operated with two, now preserved, locomotives. Perhaps the most interesting of these was an ex-South Eastern and Chatham Railway 'P' Class 0-6-0 tank engine. Photographs of both of them can be found in Chapter 8 of this book. The Bowater's railway ceased operation in October 1969 but the part of the line between Sittingbourne and Kemsley was leased to the Locomotive Club of Great Britain and the Sittingbourne & Kemsley Light Railway now operates tourist trains along it with several of the original locomotives. Other locomotives, along with additional equipment, went to create the Whipsnade & Umfolozi Railway, which is now called the Great Whipsnade Railway, at the zoo in Bedfordshire. All the locomotives, both standard and narrow gauge, that were on the system in the 1960s, with the exception of the fireless *Victor*, have been preserved.

Melior raising steam on Bowater's Sittingbourne shed. It is a 2ft 6in. gauge 'Brazil' Type outside cylinder 0-4-2 saddle tank with modified Hackworth valve gear built by Kerr, Stuart & Co. in 1924 (Works No. 4219) and it is still to be found, preserved, on the Sittingbourne & Kemsley Light Railway. *Monday 30th December 1963*

A little later that day, *Melior* was at the head of a passenger train for the workmen at Bowater's Sittingbourne. Note the spark arrestor attached to the chimney, an obvious necessity in a paper mill. These workmen's trains provided transport for employees from Sittingbourne to Kemsley Mill and Ridham Dock. Behind is 8-ton bogie pulp wagon No. 133 with wooden headstocks, built, I believe, by the locomotive manufacturer Kerr, Stuart & Co. Ltd. *30th December 1963*

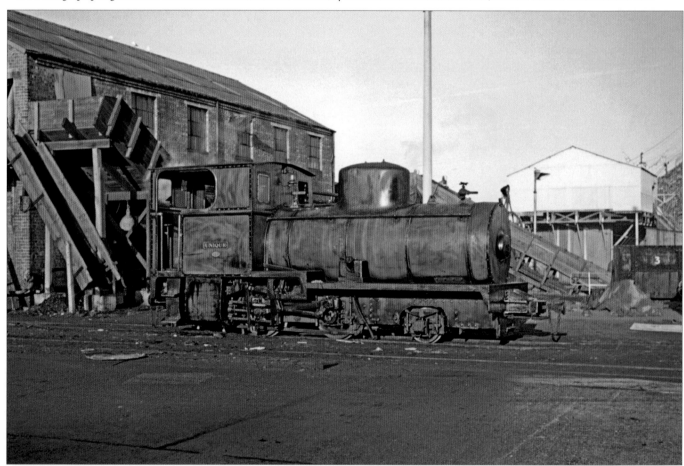

Unique, a 2-4-0 fireless locomotive built by W.G. Bagnall in 1924 (Works No. 2216), seen at Bowater's Kemsley. Like most of the Bowater's locomotives, it has been saved from the scrapman and it is now on static display at Kemsley. *Monday 30th December 1963*

Right: *Victor,* like *Unique,* was a W.G. Bagnall fireless locomotive. It was an 0-4-0 built in 1929 with the Works No. 2366. It is seen here out of steam at Bowater's Kemsley. It was cut up in 1967. It is perhaps surprising that in the combustible environment of a paper mill there were not many more fireless locomotives. *Monday 30th December 1963*

Left: *Superior* at work at Bowater's Kemsley. It is a 'Baretto' Type 0-6-2 side tank built by Kerr, Stuart for Bowater's in 1920 with the Works No. 4043. It went to the Whipsnade & Umfolozi Railway in Bedfordshire, now called the Great Whipsnade Railway, in 1970 and it is still on the two mile 2ft 6in. gauge line there. *Monday 30th December 1963*

Below: *Alpha,* a W.G. Bagnall 0-6-2 side tank built in 1932 with the Works No. 2472 takes on water at Bowater's Kemsley. It is also a 'Baretto' Type which was originally a Kerr, Stuart design but W.G. Bagnall continued production of it after Kerr, Stuart closed in 1930. *Monday 30th December 1963*

Chevallier, a Manning, Wardle 0-6-2 side tank built in 1915 with the Works No. 1877, proving it was in steam at Bowater's Ridham Dock. It was the only second-hand narrow gauge locomotive at Bowater's as it was originally the Admiralty Chattenden & Upnor Railway No. 1 which was acquired by Bowater's in 1950. *Monday 30th December 1963*

Another look at ***Alpha*** at work at Bowater's Kemsley. It was last in use in 1969 but has been preserved at the Sittingbourne & Kemsley Light Railway and is the subject of long-term restoration. Note the piles of logs behind to the right. These were transported from Ridham Dock by the overhead cableway which can be seen above the building on the left.
Monday 30th December 1963

Superb at Bowater's Ridham Dock. It is also a W.G. Bagnall 'Baretto' Type 0-6-2 side tank built in 1940 (Works No. 2624) and it has been preserved and has seen service on the Sittingbourne & Kelmsley Light Railway.
Monday 30th December 1963

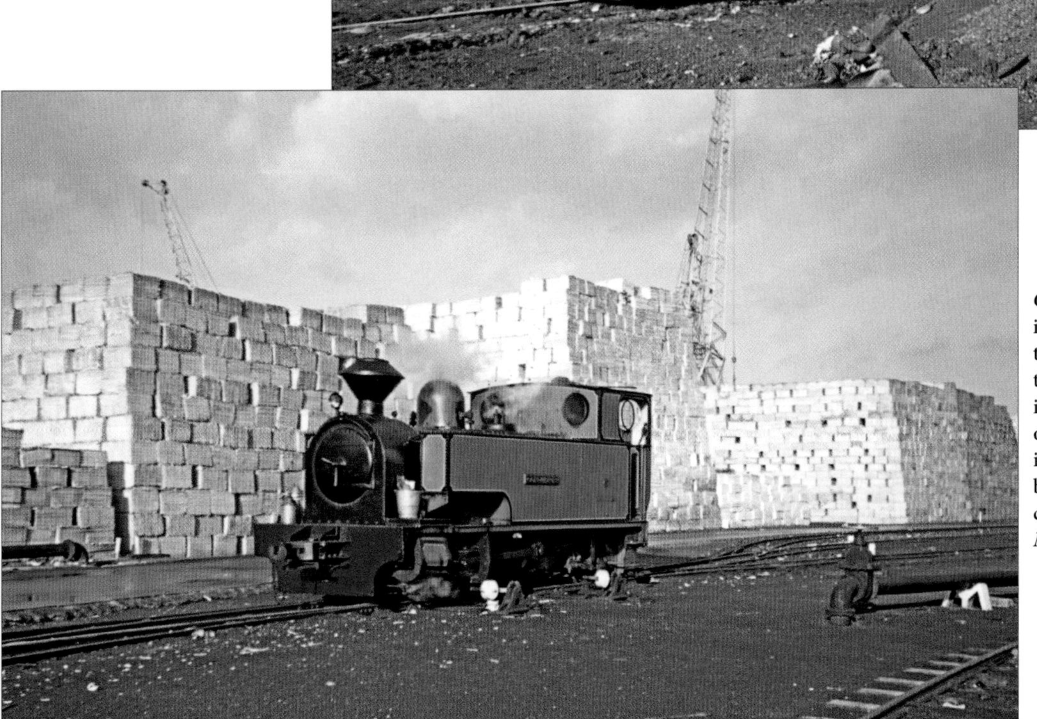

Conqueror, at Bowater's Ridham Dock, is a 1922 built W.G. Bagnall 0-6-2 side tank (Works No. 2192). It was sold to the Whipsnade and Umfolozi Railway in 1970 but it is now part of the Vale of Rheidol Railway collection which is awaiting construction of a museum building. Stacks of baled wood pulp can be seen behind.
Monday 30th December 1963

Chevallier, **the Manning, Wardle 0-6-2 side tank built in 1915 with the Works No. 1877, in a line of locomotives waiting for duty at Bowater's Ridham Dock. It was later sold to the Great Whipsnade Railway but it is no longer there and has since visited the Welshpool & Llanfair Railway.** ***Monday 30th December 1963***

Monarch **at work at Bowater's Ridham Dock. This modified Meyer articulated 0-4-4-0 side tank with four 9 x 12in. outside cylinders was built by W.G. Bagnall in 1953 with the Works No. 3024. The name was appropriate for that coronation year.** ***Monday 30th December 1963***

Several other narrow gauge industrial locomotives had already been preserved and smartened up early in the 1960s while others were still in need of attention. Three locomotives from ironstone quarries, two in Northamptonshire and one over the border in Oxfordshire, are pictured as are two others: one from a cement works and the other from a sewage treatment plan.

Cambrai, an outside cylinder 0-6-0 side tank locomotive, was built by L. Corpet of Paris in 1888 with the Works No. 493. It was originally used on the Chemin de Fer du Cambrésis in France, where it carried the name *Clary* and the number 5. In 1936 it was bought from the dealer Thom W. Ward Ltd by the Loddington Ironstone Co. Ltd in Northamptonshire and worked on the metre gauge system there until it was sold on to the Waltham Iron Ore Co. Ltd in Leicestershire in March 1956. Fortunately, in December 1960, it went to the Talyllyn Railway for preservation where it was photographed at Towyn Wharf. Appropriately, it has now returned to Northamptonshire and is on display alongside Wellingborough's metre gauge Pecketts at the Irchester Narrow Gauge Railway Museum.
Monday 28th June 1965

Another narrow gauge ironstone locomotive, *Russell*, was, like *Cambrai*, to be found preserved and on static display at Towyn in the 1960s. It is a 1ft 11½in. gauge 2-6-2 outside cylinder side tank built for the Beddgelert & South Snowdon Railway Company by the Hunslet Engine Company in 1906 with the Works No. 901. It worked on what became the Welsh Highland Railway until it was requisitioned by the Ministry of Supply for the War Effort in 1942. In the May that year it went to work at the Brymbo Steel Co. Ltd Hook Norton Ironstone Mines in Oxfordshire. In 1948 it was sold to B. Fayle & Co. Ltd Norden Clay Mines at Corfe in Dorset. In 1955 it was bought by the Birmingham Locomotive Society for £70 and moved to Towyn. After some other moves it is now to be found back home restored to working order on the Welsh Highland Heritage Railway at Gelerts Farm, Porthmadog.
Saturday 9th June 1962

Gertrude is a 2ft 0in. gauge 7 x 14in outside cylinder 0-6-0 side tank with Stephenson valve gear built by Andrew Barclay of Kilmarnock in 1918 with the Works No. 1578. It was one of three delivered new to Alfred Hickman Ltd, Sydenham Ironstone Pits, Kings Sutton, Northamptonshire. After the quarry was taken over by Stewarts & Lloyds in 1925, *Gertrude,* along with its two sisters, was sent to the Bilston Works to work the line to the melting shop. When this work ended it was bought privately and in 1960 was moved to Chipping Norton in Oxfordshire where this photograph was taken at Neville's Garage. After some later moves, it was restored at Exmoor and went to the Welsh Highland Railway to join *Russell* in 2010. More recently it has been at the Leighton Buzzard Railway.
Sunday 13th May 1962

Looking rather sorry for itself, *Mesozoic,* a 7 x 10in outside cylinder 0-6-0 saddle tank built by Peckett & Sons of Bristol in 1913 (Works No. 1327), stood rusting in the yard of P. Fenwick & Co. Ltd St. James' Works in Brackley, Northamptonshire. It had been there since July 1961 when the site was run by E.L. Pitt & Co. (Coventry) Ltd. It originally worked on the Rugby Portland Cement Co. Ltd 2ft 0in. gauge system at the Southam Works in Warwickshire. It was one of six similar Pecketts and a Bagnall 0-4-0 saddle tank which were all delivered new to Southam. There were also several petrol and diesel driven locomotives there. Four of the Pecketts were preserved. *Mesozoic* is now to be found at the Bromyard & Linton Railway in Herefordshire. The other two were scrapped as early as 1943.
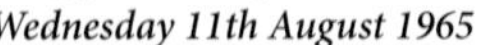
Wednesday 11th August 1965

No. 2 *Lady Luxborough,* a W.G. Bagnall 6 x 9in. outside cylinder 0-4-0 saddle tank built in 1919 (Works No. 2088), providing rides on a section of temporary track at a local fête at Hockley Heath near Birmingham. This was one of a pair of 2ft 0in. gauge Bagnall locomotives originally ordered by the Ministry of Munitions but delivered new to the Birmingham, Tame & Rea District Drainage Board when not needed at the end of the First World War.
Saturday 2nd August 1969

Although it had been taken out of service about ten years before and kept in store, No. 2 was put on sale and went to Oldberrow Vicarage Rectory, near Henley-in-Arden in Warwickshire, in 1961 where it was given its name *Lady Luxborough.* It was shown at fêtes and fairs but later sold on. In 1991 it was acquired by the Bredgar & Wormshill Light Railway in Kent and given its originally intended, but never carried, name *Armistice* and the number 4. Its sister, No. 1, Bagnall 2087 of 1918, was preserved at the Birmingham Museum of Science and Industry and given the name *Leonard.* When the museum closed, *Leonard* was moved to the Abbey Pumping Station industrial museum in Leicester.

The First Garratt

The first 'Garratt' Type locomotive to be built, by Beyer, Peacock & Co. in 1909 (Works No. 5292), was 'K1' for the 2ft gauge North East Dundas Tramway in Tasmania. When no longer required, it was placed in store and Beyer, Peacock bought it in 1947 for display at the Gorton Works in Manchester. Apparently it had a number of replacement parts cannibalised from sister locomotive 'K2'. With the imminent closure of the works, it was placed on display at Porthmadog Harbour station on the Ffestiniog Railway where it had recently arrived when photographed. By the following year it was in store out of sight at Boston Lodge Works where it stayed until 1976 when it went on loan to the National Railway Museum at York until 1995. The reopening of the Welsh Highland Railway meant there was a suitable line for it to run on and it was restored, at Tyseley, Boston Lodge and Dinas, over a number of years and returned to steam in 2004 and then, after a few problems, used in service two years later. After a period of time out of use when its boiler ticket expired it went to the Statfold Barn Railway where it was returned to full working order. *Sunday 10th April 1966*

Part Two: Scotland

Scottish Gas Board Aberdeen Gas Works *Mr Therm* and *City of Aberdeen*. *Wednesday 28th August 1963*

My first vivid memory of steam in Scotland was in 1959 when I was thirteen and my father, who was from Dumbarton, took me to see the beauty of the Highlands and Islands. This was quite a contrast to mountainless Warwickshire and it was an exciting trip for me. On the train from Mallaig to Fort William, after visiting the Isle of Skye, he must have been very pleased to hear me cry out: *"Just look at those lochs!"*, but the lochs which had excited me were not the local watery kind but *Loch Rannoch* and *Loch Arkaig*, ex-Great Northern Railway 'H3', London and North Eastern Railway 'K2', Class 2-6-0s double-heading the train. Unfortunately, the only photographs I took were in grainy black and white with my trusty Kodak Brownie camera.

Some years later, in August 1963 while I was waiting for my O-level results, in possession of a £5.5s 0d week-long Freedom of Scotland Rail Rover and armed with some precious colour slide film, I set off north by bus with fellow enthusiast Mike Collins. Once in the Scottish Region we visited many British Railways engine sheds, of course, sleeping on trains as much as possible on the longest available overnight run within the geographical limit of the Rover. This was not a problem going north but on one occasion, after oversleeping, we had to jump down onto the track at an unscheduled stop at Carnforth and hitch back to Rover valid territory at Carlisle from the end of what was then called the Lancaster bypass, one of Britain's first motorways.

We wanted to satisfy our interest in industrial systems as well and we were not disappointed. During the first half of the the 1960s Scotland still provided a wide range of industrial steam environments ranging from smoky and polluted industrial sites, such as Bairds and Scottish Steel Gartsherrie Works with its fleet of nineteenth and early twentieth century locomotives, through gas works, power stations and collieries to interesting street running in Aberdeen and glorious rural scenery at the National Coal Board Waterside system and at the Balmenach Distillery near Granton-on-Spey. Not surprisingly, many of the locomotives had been built by Scottish companies. A large number were Andrew Barclay products from the Caledonia Works in Kilmarnock. These were mainly saddle tanks but there were also some side tanks. I was fascinated to see unusual examples still in steam from other Scottish manufacturers including Grant, Ritchie & Co. of Kilmarnock and Gibb and Hogg, Victoria Engine Works in Airdrie. Of particular interest

No. 21 hard at work. It was allocated to the Waterside system for its entire working life until it was transferred to Cairnhill Colliery at the end of 1973. The train had ten 16-ton British Railway mineral wagons followed by a number of internal use wooden sided wagons bound for the washery. ***Friday 16th April 1965***

were locomotives from three connected producers: Neilson & Co. Springburn Works in Glasgow which became Neilson Reid & Co. Ltd in 1898 and part of the North British Locomotive Co. Ltd of Glasgow in 1903. Several of these were in action at the Bairds and Scottish Steel works at Gartsherrie, Coatbridge, in Lanarkshire which we briefly squeezed in between visits to Eastfield, Motherwell and Kipps BR sheds on Saturday 24th August 1963. I clearly remember that this was the day after the Beatles single *She Loves You* was released.

We decided that as more time was needed to appreciate the elderly saddle tanks we found there we would make a point of returning again the following Friday when we also found a rare Gibb and Hogg 'ogee' saddle tank working hard at the neighbouring Bairds and Scottish Steel works at Northburn. It looked in a very sorry state but despite that it seems to have lasted in service for a little longer as it was not scrapped until 1965. Other 'finds' at collieries were unusual 0-4-2 saddle tanks and an Andrew Barclay 'ogee' tank. A rare 'sassenach' away from home was the immaculately clean Black, Hawthorn & Co. Ltd of Gateshead *City of Aberdeen* in the Granite City. We found it inside the engine shed at the gas works and the friendly and helpful crew of Andrew Barclay locomotive *Mr Therm* hauled it out for us to photograph before taking a train of wagons through the streets to the docks. Fortunately, along with several other locomotives in this book, these Aberdeen locomotives have been preserved.

A couple of years later main line attention had turned to the remaining 'A4' Pacifics which were employed at that time on the three-hour Aberdeen to Glasgow expresses. There was also a handful of other classes still active but the great attraction was the use of four pre-grouping locomotives in their original liveries which hauled a number of special excursions to mark the impending demise of steam. This tempted us north of the border on several occasions and provided the opportunity to further indulge our interest in industrial systems with visits to the Balmenach Distillery line, collieries and gas works as well as a very welcome return to the Waterside system centred on the Dunaskin shed.

Chapter 10

The National Coal Board Waterside System in Ayrshire

The extensive Waterside system served several collieries in the upper Doon Valley in Ayrshire. The engine shed, workshops and washery were situated at Dunaskin and part of the site became the Scottish Industrial Railway Centre, now known as the Doon Valley Railway. The system had provided coal to the Dalmellington Iron Company works until that closed down in 1921 but the railway and washery continued to serve the collieries at Pennyvenie, Minnivey and Houldsworth and link them to the British Railways ex-Glasgow & South Western Railway Dalmellington branch at Cutler Sidings until they were progressively closed in the 1970s. The last mine to close was Pennyvenie in 1978 although there was later development of opencast mining at nearby Chalmerston.

The mines had become part of Bairds and Dalmellington Ltd in 1931 and, along with other colliery companies, they were nationalised in 1947. It had initially been in the NCB Scottish West Ayr Area 5 which had become area 'Ay' by the time of the photographs.

Left: No. 17, a 45-ton 0-6-0 side tank locomotive with 18 x 24in. outside cylinders and 3ft 9in. driving wheels, working on the NCB Waterside system. It was built by Andrew Barclay of Kilmarnock and delivered new to the Dalmellington Iron Company in 1913, Works No. 1338. As was the general practice on this system, it had an open fronted coal wagon attached for use as a tender for the long runs up to Pennyvenie, Minnivey and Houldsworth collieries.
Monday 26th August 1963

Below: Nineteen months later, No. 17 was still hard at work, again attached to the open fronted coal wagon in use as a tender. It had the Railway Executive registration No. 469 of 1952 so that it could work in the British Railways exchange sidings on the ex-Glasgow & South Western Railway Dalmellington branch.
Friday 16th April 1965

Another view of No. 17 at NCB Waterside on its train of Hudson tipper wagons in early morning sunshine. The tippers were used to take spoil to Cutler Tip between Dunaskin and Minnivey.
Friday 16th April 1965

A short time later, No. 17 was in charge of a fully loaded train of seven plank wooden NCB coal trucks for internal use from Pennyvenie or Minnivey Colliery to the Dunaskin Washery. No. 17 was transferred to the Cowdenbeath Central Workshops in Fife just before the closure of the Waterside system in July 1978 and then went on to the Withdrawn Machinery Stores at Arniston, Midlothian, for storage in March 1979. In October 1980 it was saved for preservation and placed in store at the Tanfield Railway. *Friday 16th April 1965*

Fifteen minutes after No. 17 had passed by it was followed by No. 22 hauling a train of loaded British Railways 16-ton mineral wagons. This was another Andrew Barclay 0-6-0 side tank locomotive with 18 x 24in. outside cylinders. It was built in 1923 with the Works No. 1785 and delivered new to the Dalmellington Iron Company. It was scrapped in September 1969. *Friday 16th April 1965*

No. 23, an outside cylinder 0-4-0 saddle tank built by Grant, Richie & Co. in 1911 with the Works No. 531, out of steam at Dunaskin. It was particularly interesting because it had retained its wooden block dumb buffers. It had originally worked at Baird's Eglinton Ironworks with the name ***Eglinton No.6*** but had arrived at Waterside in 1931. *Monday 26th August 1963*

Despite the impression given twenty months earlier, the Grant, Richie & Co. No. 23 is seen here very much in action on the NCB Waterside system. After a couple of moves to other collieries it was scrapped at Killoch Colliery towards the end of 1971. *Friday 16th April 1965*

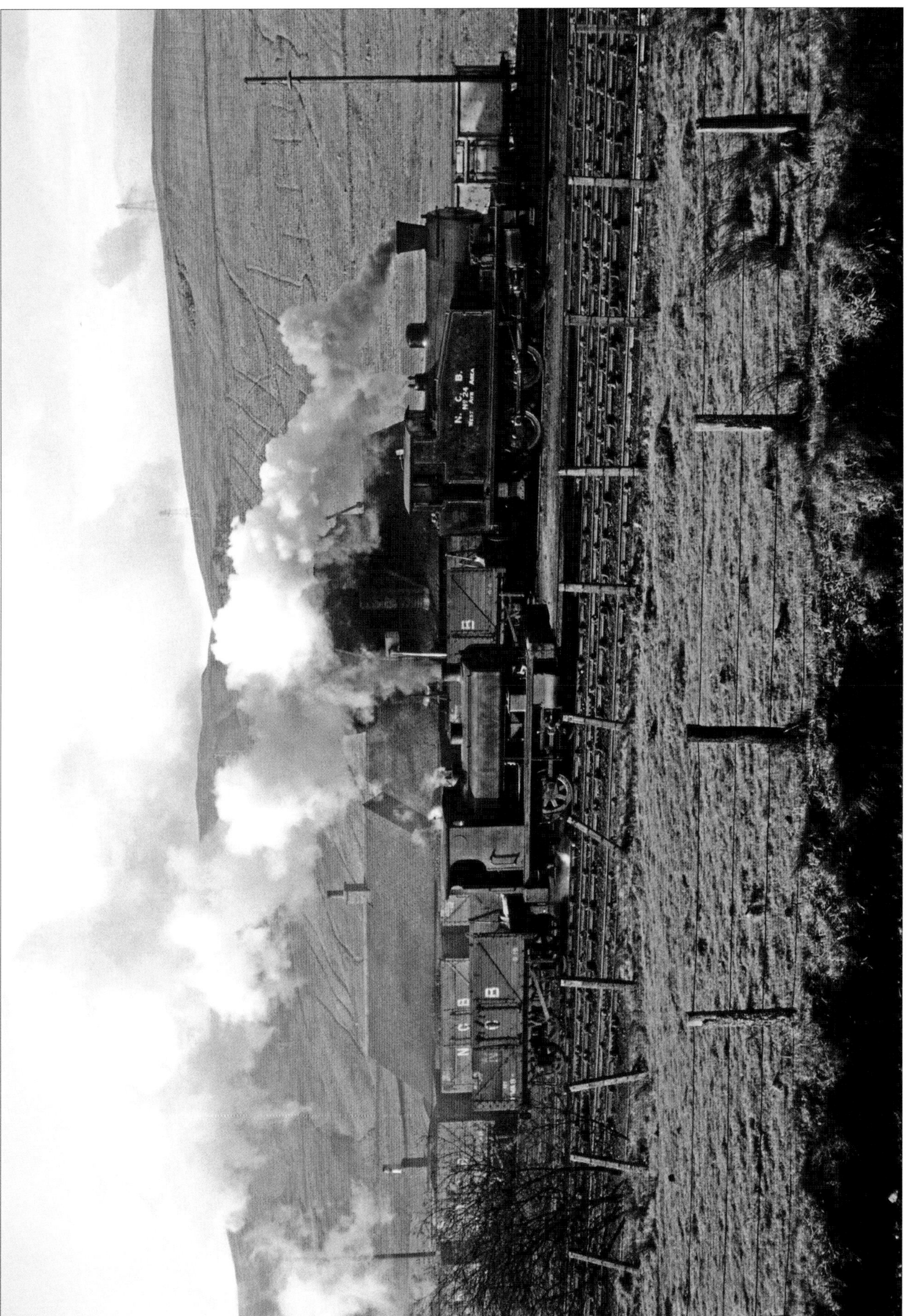

The Grant, Ritchie & Co. No. 23 is seen running alongside No. 24, an 18 x 24in. outside cylinder 0-6-0 side tank locomotive built by Andrew Barclay in 1953 with the Works No. 2335, by the bothy at Cutler Sidings. No. 24 had been delivered new to the NCB Waterside system and was previously numbered 8. Its original chimney had been replaced with a Giesl ejector. It is now preserved and owned by the Royal Museum of Scotland and is on loan to the Bo'ness & Kinneil Railway with its later number, 24. *Friday 16th April 1965*

On the same day, No. 23 hauled a fully loaded train past St. Francis Xavier's Church and the single storey cottages of Chapel Row, all on the opposite side of the main A713 Dalmellington Road. A spoil tip, called a 'bing' in Scotland, can be seen in the distance. *Friday 16th April 1965*

LEFT: Now preserved at the Scottish Industrial Railway Centre at Dunaskin, No. 1 is a 16 x 24in. outside cylinder Andrew Barclay 0-4-0 saddle tank built in 1947 with the Works No. 2244 and delivered new to Waterside. It is seen here at work at Cutler Sidings. Later renumbered 10, it was in service until Pennyvenie Colliery and the system closed in 1978.
Monday 26th August 1963

BELOW: No. 19 is a 16 x 24in. outside cylinder 0-4-0 saddle tank built by Andrew Barclay and delivered new in 1918 with the Works No. 1614. The engine is also now at the Doon Valley Railway at Dunaskin.
Friday 16th April 1965

No. 14 was an 0-4-0 outside cylinder saddle tank built by Andrew Barclay in 1906 for the Dalmellington Iron Co. Ltd with the Works No. 1062. It is seen here at NCB Waterside. It had 16 x 24in. cylinders and 3ft 7in. driving wheels. It was scrapped in March 1965.
Monday 26th August 1963

No. 18, an Andrew Barclay 0-6-0 side tank built in 1930 with the Works No. 1985, seen here at Waterside. New to the Coltness Iron Company, New Mains, Lanarkshire, where it was No. 3, it had moved to Waterside in January 1955 and it was eventually scrapped there in September 1965. Rare for Barclay, this was one of a small number of inside cylinder tank locomotives built by that manufacturer. It had 18 x 26in. cylinders and large 4ft 3in. driving wheels.
Monday 26th August 1963

No. 21, a 16 x 24in outside cylinder 0-4-0 saddle tank, was built by Andrew Barclay in 1949 with the Works No. 2284. The crew looked happy despite the 'dreich' weather. This photograph shows that the open fronted coal wagons used as tenders remained attached to the locomotives and not to the coal trains.
Monday 26th August 1963

A second view of No. 21, but in much better weather on Friday 16th April 1965. The two tall chimneys of the Dunaskin Brickworks, which was built on the site of the defunct Dalmellington Iron Company ironworks and opened in 1928, can be seen on the right. Production ended in 1976. After it was taken out of service No. 21 was exhibited at the National Mining Museum of Scotland at Lady Victoria Colliery, Newtongrange, Midlothian.

Most of the coal was, of course, taken away by British Railways. Ex-London Midland & Scottish Railway No. 42780, a Hughes designed 'Crab' 2-6-0 built at Crewe Works as LM&SR No. 13080 in 1927, crosses Burton (sometimes referred to as Dalrymple) Viaduct on an empty coal train on the Dalmellington branch in Ayrshire. The locomotive was allocated to Ayr shed (67C) at the time. Passenger services on the Dalmellington branch had ended in April the previous year but coal output at the NCB Waterside Colliery and, more recently, traffic from the Chalmerston open cast mine meant that much of the branch remained open. *Friday 16th April 1965*

Chapter 11

National Coal Board Scottish Collieries

Knockshinnoch Castle and Bank Collieries, Ayrshire

Apart from the impressive Waterside system there were, of course, dozens of collieries in Scotland. Knockshinnoch Castle Colliery, linked to Bank Colliery, was not far from Waterside. It had been in the NCB Scottish East Ayr Area 8 which had become area 'Ay' by the time of the photographs.

This colliery, which closed in 1968, was the site of the Knockshinnoch Disaster in 1950 when more than a hundred miners were trapped underground by flooding and, sadly, thirteen died. It was the theme of the 1952 film *The Brave Don't Cry* starring John Gregson. Locomotives were based at the connected Bank Colliery.

No. 8, a 16 x 24in. outside cylinder Andrew Barclay 0-4-0 saddle tank built in 1955 with the Works No. 2369, hard at work at Knockshinnoch Castle Colliery in Ayrshire on a train of Hudson tipper wagons in interesting early morning light.
Friday 16th April 1965

No. 8 crosses a traditional gated level crossing at Knockshinnoch Castle Colliery. It had started its working life at Bank Colliery and spent some time at Lugar and Kames collieries but at the time of this photograph it had been allocated again to Bank Colliery, linked to Castle Colliery. It went on to Barony Colliery in 1968 and was sold for preservation in 1982. It was at the Derwent Valley Light Railway near York until 2017 when it went to the Appleby Frodingham Railway Preservation Society based at Scunthorpe Steelworks.
Friday 16th April 1965

The Arniston Withdrawn Machinery Store at Gorebridge, Midlothian

The Arniston Withdrawn Machinery Store at Gorebridge was on the site of the ex-Arniston Coal Co. Ltd Colliery which had closed on 29th April 1962 and it was host to a number of locomotives which, as its name implied, were surplus to requirements. It was in the NCB Lothians Area.

There was an unusual veteran Andrew Barclay 12 x 20in. outside cylinder 0-4-0 'ogee' Type saddle tank locomotive built in 1881 with the Works No. 224 at the recently opened Arniston Withdrawn Machinery Store at Gorebridge. It had worked at the Summerlee Iron Company Mossend Ironworks near Motherwell and at the same company's Prestongrange Colliery as No 8. Prestongrange closed at the end of 1962 and, now numbered 22, the locomotive had made its way to Arniston just a couple of months before this photograph was taken. *Thursday 29th August 1963*

Another view of Andrew Barclay Works No. 224 of 1881 at Arniston. There was, apparently, an attempt to preserve this interesting locomotive but, sadly, it was not successful. It is clear from the name of the site that the equipment was considered to be withdrawn so the possibility that a locomotive found there would be placed back in service was very remote. It is doubtful if AB 224 steamed again because it was scrapped early in 1964. *Thursday 29th August 1963*

No. 16 was an outside cylinder 0-4-0 saddle tank built by Andrew Barclay with the Works No. 158. New to Niddrie & Benhar Coal Co. Ltd in 1875, where it was named ***Niddrie No. 1.*** It was rebuilt by Andrew Barclay in 1908 (Works No. 9221). This likely explains why, though older than Andrew Barclay Works No. 224 built in 1881, it had the recognisable saddle tanks of that company rather than 'ogee' tanks. After nationalisation it was allocated to a number of collieries in the NCB Area 2 of East Lothian and Midlothian. On Thursday 29th August 1963 it was at the Arniston Withdrawn Machinery Store and it was scrapped the following year. *Thursday 29th August 1963*

No. 26 was a 14 x 22in. outside cylindered 0-4-0 saddle tank with 3ft 5in. wheels built by Andrew Barclay for Edinburgh Collieries Ltd in 1902 with the Works No. 930. It was rebuilt by Hawthorns of Leith in 1924. It was originally allocated to Carberry Colliery where it was named ***Carberry***. It had been transferred to Arniston shortly before this photograph was taken, but its time there was short as it was scrapped early in 1964.
Thursday 29th August 1963

No. 30 seen here also at the Arniston Withdrawn Machinery Store. It was an Andrew Barclay outside cylinder 0-4-0 saddle tank built in 1938 with the Works No. 2058. It had entered service new as No. 6 with Edinburgh Collieries Ltd. After serving time at Meadowhill, Fleets and Niddrie collieries it was transferred to Arniston Colliery shortly before this photograph was taken. It looked in a sorry state without its coupling rods so it is probable it did not work again as it was scrapped the following year. The sign on the building on the far left reads 'Civil Defence Centre', a reminder that this was during the Cold War. *Sunday 18th April 1965*

Newbattle Central Workshops and Lady Victoria Colliery, Newtongrange, Midlothian

Newbattle Central Workshops and the adjacent former Lothian Coal Co. Ltd Lady Victoria Colliery were at Newtongrange, not far from Edinburgh, in the NCB Lothians Area. Much of the site survives as the present-day National Mining Museum Scotland. The rail connection was with the ex-North British Railway line from Edinburgh to Carlisle, better known as the Waverley Route, on the part which has now reopened. Lady Victoria Colliery, named after the wife of the chairman, was in operation until 1981.

No. 5 was an outside cylinder saddle tank with the rare 0-4-2 wheel arrangement built by Grant, Ritchie & Co. in 1908 with the Works No. 527. It was delivered new to the Lothian Coal Company at Lady Victoria Colliery where it was rebuilt in 1933. It spent its entire working life there except for around four months at the time this photograph was taken, when it was at Newbattle Central Workshops. It was scrapped at Lady Victoria Colliery in August 1969.
Thursday 29th August 1963

No. 3 is Andrew Barclay 0-6-0 saddle tank 1458 of 1916, with 16 x 22in. outside cylinders, built for the Ministry of Munitions, Houston, Georgetown, near Paisley. When no longer required after the First World War, in 1919, it was sold to the Lothian Coal Company and worked at Lady Victoria Colliery at Newtongrange. It remained there except for a three year stay at Newbattle Shops that ended soon after this photograph was taken, and a later, final, return to Newbattle. Fortunately No. 3 was donated for preservation by the NCB and displayed at the 1988 Glasgow Garden Festival painted yellow with the name ***Lady Victoria.*** After some time at the Scottish Railway Preservation Society site at Bo'ness, it is now back home at Newtongrange on long term loan as an exhibit in the National Mining Museum Scotland.
Thursday 29th August 1963

No. 21 was a 16 x 24in. outside cylinder 0-6-0 saddle tank built by Andrew Barclay with the Works No. 2026 and delivered new to the Niddrie & Benhar Coal Co. Ltd in 1937. Originally named ***Niddrie No 7***, it spent most of its working life at the NCB Niddrie sheds where it was finally cut up in September 1969. It is seen in this photograph during a short stay at the NCB Newbattle Shops. *Thursday 29th August 1963*

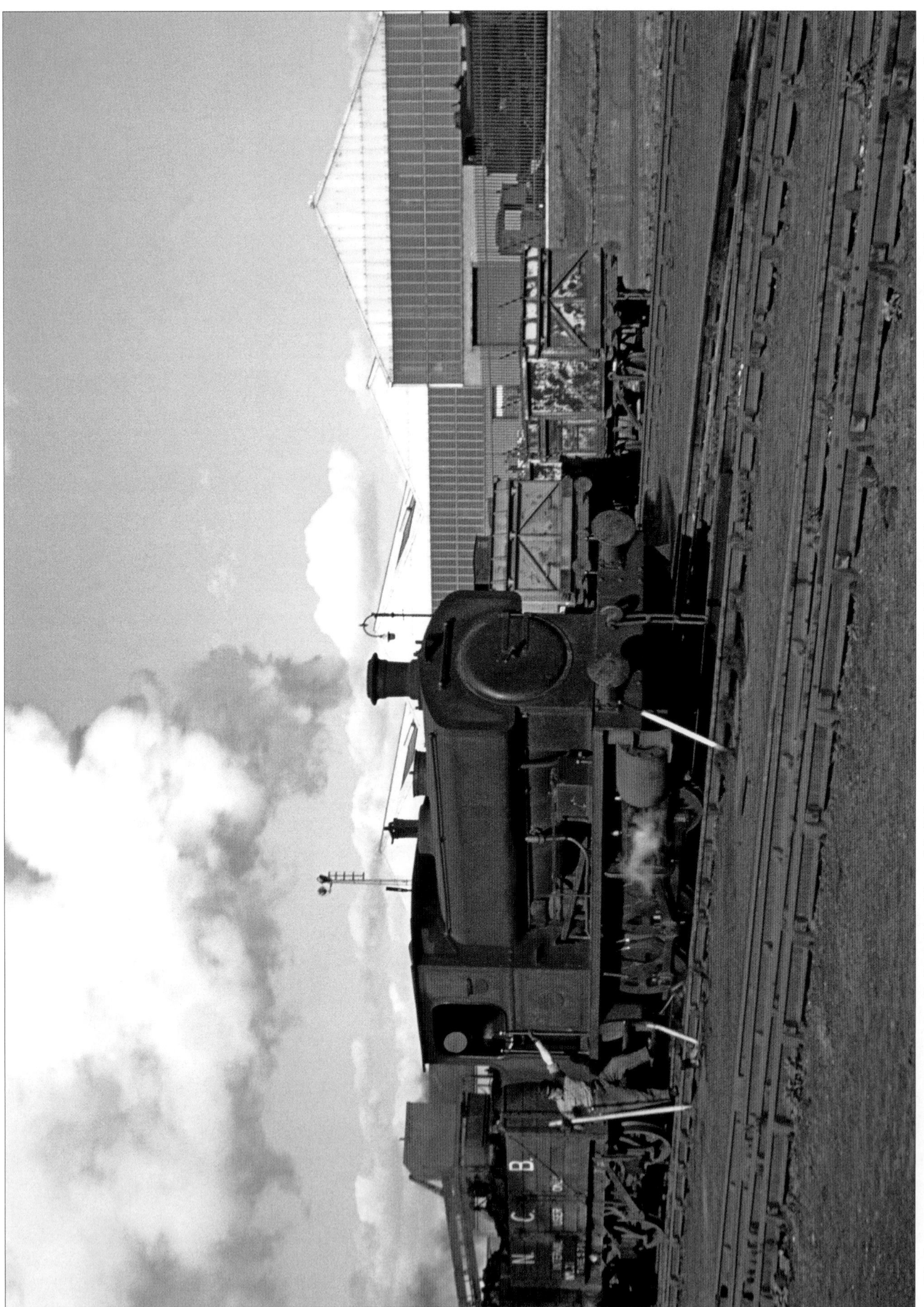

No. 8, now preserved, is a 15 x 20in. outside cylinder 0-6-0 saddle tank built by Andrew Barclay with the Works No. 1175. Seen here working at Lady Victoria Colliery. Delivered new to the Arniston Coal Company in 1909 as No. 5, it became No. 8 after nationalisation and it was transferred from Arniston Colliery to Lady Victoria Colliery in the early 1950s. *Thursday 29th August 1963*

No. 8 shunting at Lady Victoria Colliery. This locomotive is now called ***Dardanelles,*** the local name for Polkemmet Colliery to where it was transferred in 1973, and it is on static display at the Polkemmet Country Park in West Lothian. *Thursday 29th August 1963*

No. 31 was a 14 x 22in. outside cylinder Andrew Barclay 0-4-0 saddle tank with the Works No. 2146 seen here working at Lady Victoria Colliery. It had been supplied new to the Ormiston Coal Company Ltd Limeylands Colliery in 1942. It moved on to Meadowmill Colliery, East Lothian, the year after this photograph was taken and it was withdrawn early in 1970. *Thursday 29th August 1963*

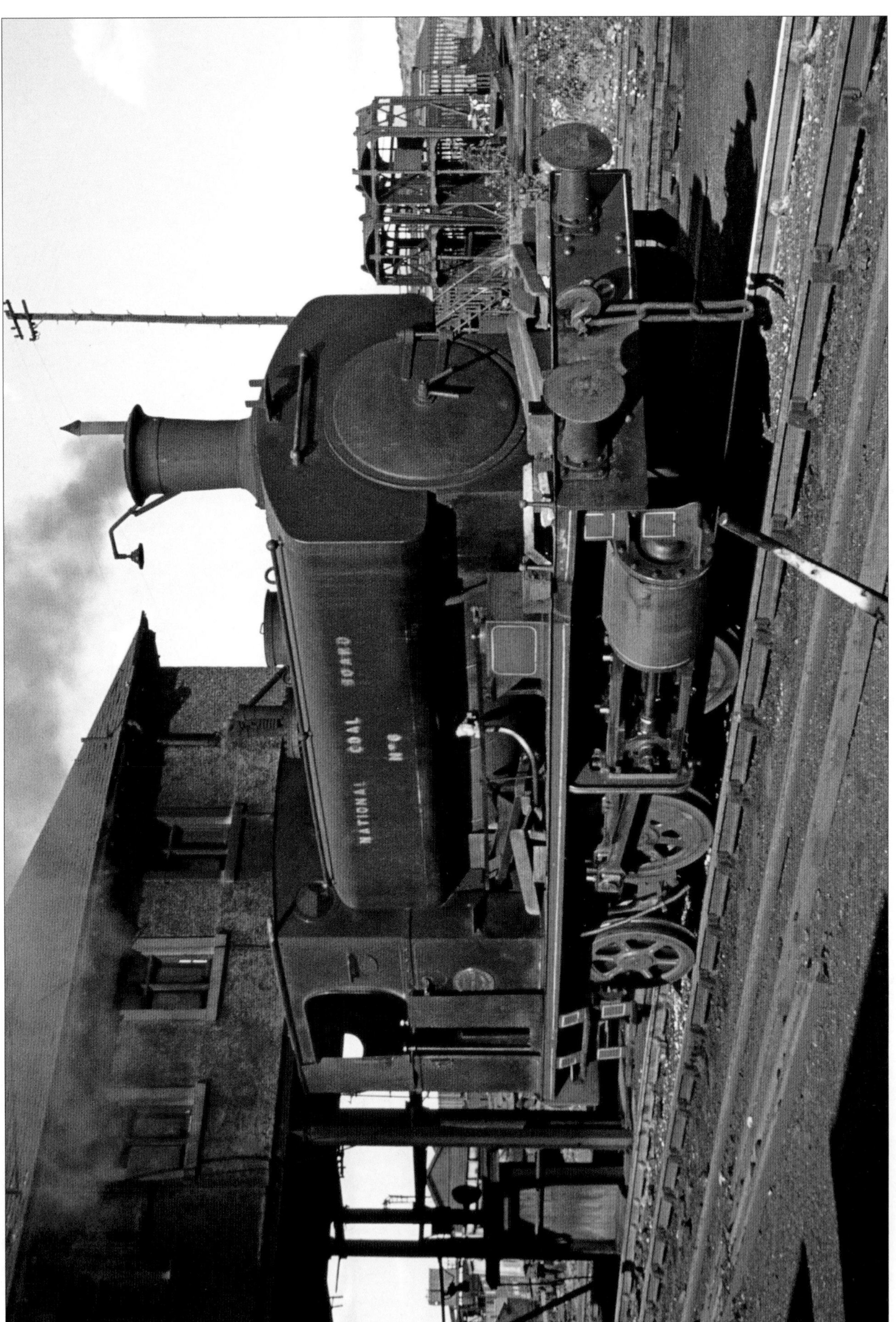

No. 6, seen here at Lady Victoria Colliery, was a 15 x 22in. outside cylinder Andrew Barclay product built for the Lothian Coal Company Ltd in 1910 with the Works No. 1193. It had the relatively uncommon 0-4-2 wheel arrangement with 3ft 6in. driving wheels. Fortunately, it is now preserved at the Tanfield Railway. There were three 0-4-2 saddle tanks at Lady Victoria: the Barclay (I believe there were only two from that manufacturer in Scotland and that the other one had been scrapped in 1960) and two by the other Kilmarnock engine builder, Grant, Ritchie & Co. One of these is preserved at the Prestongrange Mining Museum at Prestonpans. *Thursday 29th August 1963*

Kinneil Colliery, Bo'ness, West Lothian

The ex-Kinneil Cannel & Coking Coal Co. Ltd Kinneil Colliery at Bo'ness in West Lothian was connected to the ex-Slamannan and Borrowstounness Railway, later North British Railway, branch from Bo'ness Junction at Manuel to Bridgeness on the River Forth. It was in the NCB Scottish Division Alloa Area. The colliery closed in 1982 but the Scottish Railway Preservation Society's Bo'ness & Kinneil Railway Kinneil station has been built by the landscaped former colliery site.

No. 4 in steam at Kinneil Colliery. It was a 16 x 24in. outside cylinder 0-4-0 saddle tank built by Andrew Barclay in 1949 with the Works No. 2259. It first went to Devon Colliery in Clackmannanshire and, after several moves, had arrived at Kinneil Colliery just four months before this photograph was taken. It left Kinneil for Cowdenbeath Central Workshops in 1967 and it later worked at Manor Powis Colliery. It had been renumbered 30 when it was finally withdrawn from Frances Colliery, Fife, and it is now on display at the Lochore Meadows Country Park in Fife. *Tuesday 27th August 1963*

No. 31 at Kinneil Colliery. It was a Grant, Richie & Co. outside cylinder 0-4-0 saddle tank built in 1905 with the Works No. 480. It was originally owned by the Fife Coal Company as number 4 and was based at Mary Colliery, Lochore, where it spent most of its working life well into National Coal Board times. It had been transferred to Kinneil just a few months before this photograph was taken. *Tuesday 27th August 1963*

Nearly two years later, the Grant, Richie No. 31 was still at Kinneil Colliery looking well cared for but it was scrapped on site the month after this photograph was taken. *Sunday 18th April 1965*

Cowdenbeath Central Workshops, Fife

The Cowdenbeath Central Workshops were built in 1924 by the Fife Coal Company Ltd. Here equipment was stored and material was constructed and maintained. It became the NCB area offices and central works for the Fife and Clackmannan Area.

No. 24, an Andrew Barclay outside cylinder saddle tank built in 1894 with the Works No. 727, had clearly been withdrawn from service when seen here at Cowdenbeath Central Workshops. It had previously worked from new at the Lochgelly Iron and Coal Co. Ltd Jenny Gray Colliery until it moved to Lumphinnans No. 11 colliery around 1955. A further move to Cowdenbeath Central Workshops around two years before this photograph was taken does not seem to have ended well because it was scrapped in May 1966. Another unidentified Barclay in similar condition was behind. *Tuesday 27th August 1963*

Chapter 12

Iron and Steel, Power Production and a Distillery

Bairds & Scottish Steel Northburn Works and Gartsherrie Works, Coatbridge, Lanarkshire

Bairds & Scottish Steel was formed in 1938 by the merger of William Baird & Co. Ltd which had been established at Gartsherrie in Coatbridge in 1830 and the Scottish Iron & Steel Co. Ltd. It was then nationalised under the Iron and Steel Act and became part of the Iron & Steel Corporation of Great Britain on the Vesting Date: 15th February 1951. The management did not really change but when the industry was de-nationalised Bairds did not purchase it back and it was bought by a consortium around the time of my visit in 1963. However, the company was unable to make the Gartsherrie Works viable and it was closed, along with the neighbouring B&SS Northburn Works at Kipps which apparently lasted for a few months longer under different ownership, in 1967 and so it did not become part of the British Steel Corporation on re-nationalisation of the industry that year.

Bairds & Scottish Steel No. 2 hard at work at the B&SS Northburn Works. It was an outside cylinder 0-4-0 'ogee' saddle tank built by Gibb & Hogg at the Victoria Engine Works in Airdrie and it had first worked at the Globe Ironworks at Motherwell and then at the North British Ironworks at Coatbridge but it had moved to Northburn before the Second World War. Its bent running plate and handrail, as well as its unkempt, filthy condition, suggested it was nearing the end of its working days and, sadly, this interesting and unusual locomotive was scrapped in 1965.
Friday 30th August 1963

Another look at Bairds & Scottish Steel No. 2, the rare 0-4-0 'ogee' saddle tank, in action at the Northburn works. It has been recorded as built in 1915 but other sources say that Gibb & Hogg ceased locomotive construction around 1911 after building only about twenty which probably had tanks similar in outline to the familiar Andrew Barclay products. It is possible that it was much older and had been rebuilt in 1915 but it seems highly unlikely to have been a major rebuild changing from regular tanks to 'ogee' tanks at that date. It could have been an early Gibb and Hogg and had always been fitted with these tanks or another possibility might be that the tanks needed replacing and a cheap solution was to cannibalise some from another locomotive from a different manufacturer.
Friday 30th August 1963

The oldest resident at the Gartsherrie Works in 1963 was No. 11, a 14 x 20in. outside cylinder 0-4-0 saddle tank with 3ft 8in. wheels built by Neilson & Co. in 1882 with the Works No. 2937. It first worked at Bedley Colliery, which belonged to Bairds & Scottish Steel, but this was nationalised along with the other collieries in 1947. No 11 continued to work at the then National Coal Board Bedlay Colliery for a couple of years before returning to Bairds' ownership at the Gartsherrie Works where it was photographed. Fortunately it went to the Railway Preservation Society at Hednesford for preservation in June 1968 and it is now to be found on the Chasewater Railway. *Friday 30th August 1963*

No. 3 was a 14 x 20in. outside cylinder 0-4-0 saddle tank built by Neilson & Co. in 1887 with the Works No. 3629. The second oldest locomotive at Bairds & Scottish Steel's Gartsherrie Works when photographed, it was just five years younger than No. 11. It also worked at times at the B&SS Northburn Works and was scrapped in 1968. *Friday 30th August 1963*

No. 5, a third veteran 0-4-0 outside cylinder saddle tank built by Neilson & Co. in 1889, with the Works No. 3994, hard at work at the Bairds & Scottish Steel Gartsherrie Works. It was scrapped five years later, in August 1968, the same month that the 'fifteen guinea special' marking the end of main line steam ran on British Railways. *Friday 30th August 1963*

A fourth 19th century 14 x 20in. outside cylinder 0-4-0 saddle tank at the Gartsherrie Works that day was No. 6 which was built by Neilson, Reid Co. Ltd in 1899 with the Works No. 5566. This marked a change because Neilson & Co. had become Neilson, Reid & Co. Ltd in 1898. No. 6 was transferred to the Northburn Works three months after this photograph was taken and it was scrapped in April 1964. *Friday 30th August 1963*

Bairds & Scottish Steel 0-4-0 saddle tank No. 19 had slightly larger 15 x 20in. outside cylinders, 3ft 9in. wheels and a different, more enclosed, cab design. It was built in 1908 with the Works No. 18385 at the Neilson, Reid Hyde Park works although by this time the manufacturer had become the North British Locomotive Co. after the merger of Neilson, Reid with Sharp, Stewart and Dübs & Co. in 1903. Seen here in action at the Gartsherrie Works where it had spent all its working life. It was scrapped in August 1968.
Saturday 24th August 1963

The following week, No. 19 was in action again at the Gartsherrie Works. The North British Locomotive Company products closely resembled the earlier Neilson ones though with a visibly different cab design. *Friday 30th August 1963*

Bairds & Scottish Steel No. 20 was also at work at the Gartsherrie Works that day. Like No. 19, it was a 15 x 20in. outside cylinder 0-4-0 saddle tank built by the North British Locomotive Co. at the Hyde Park works in 1908. It had the Works No. 18386 and, like its sister, it was delivered new to Gartsherrie but it had a happier fate because when it was withdrawn it went to the now closed Lytham Motive Power Museum, Lancashire. It later moved to Helical Technology, Lytham St. Annes.
Friday 30th August 1963

Bairds & Scottish Steel No. 4, an 0-4-0 outside cylinder saddle tank built by Andrew Barclay in 1917 with the Works No. 1481, at the Gartsherrie Works. It had just been rebuilt using parts of a 1916 built Andrew Barclay locomotive with the Works No. 1467 and was in a remarkably clean condition when compared to the other locomotives at the site. It was destined for service at the B&SS Northburn Works where it was eventually scrapped in March 1968. Like the North British family it had dumb buffers. *Friday 30th August 1963*

Not strictly an industrial railway locomotive but interesting in the context. This 14 x 20in. outside cylinder 0-4-0 saddle tank locomotive was very similar to the Gartsherrie locomotives and resided at the nearby British Railways Scottish Region Kipps motive power depot, which had been coded 65E but had recently become a sub-shed of Eastfield (65A). The North British Railway, not to be confused with the North British Locomotive Co. Ltd, bought two Neilson built locomotives and then constructed thirty-four more of the type at their own Cowlairs Works. BR No. 68104 was built at Cowlairs in 1890 as North British Railway 'G' Class, later L&NER 'Y9' Class, number 9009. Its cab resembled the later slightly more enclosed North British Locomotive Co. Ltd design and, when in service, many of the class were attached to wooden tenders. No. 68104, had already been withdrawn, in October 1962, when it was seen at Kipps. This was the day after the Beatles single *She Loves You* was released. I believe it was the last of the class in existence with the exception of 68095 (NBR 42) which has been preserved and is now to be found as a static exhibit at the Scottish Railway Preservation Society museum at Bo'ness. Unfortunately No. 68104 was cut up shortly after this photograph was taken. *Saturday 24th August 1963*

The South of Scotland Electricity Board, Yoker Power Station, Glasgow

The coal-fired Yoker Power Station was opened in 1905 and was acquired by the Clyde Valley Electric Power Co. which was nationalised in 1948. Yoker was then operated by the South West Scotland Electricity Board which was a division of the British Electricity Authority. The SWSEB later became part of the South of Scotland Electricity Board (SSEB) as the result of re-organisation. Yoker Power Station was closed in 1976.

South of Scotland Electricity Board No. 4, an 0-4-0 saddle tank with 14 x 22in. outside cylinders built by Andrew Barclay with the Works No. 2047, was delivered new to the Clyde Valley Electrical Power Co. Yoker Power Station in Glasgow in 1937. It was the only steam locomotive there when photographed. ***Saturday 24th August 1963***

No. 4 shunting at Yoker Power Station. It was bought for a railway project in the Orkney Islands some time after withdrawal from service in the 1970s. When this plan fell through it was moved to the East Somerset Railway at Cranmore and restored to look like an ex Swansea Harbour Trust locomotive absorbed into the Great Western Railway in 1923. It was given the fictitious GWR number 705 and first painted GWR green and later BR black. It was put up for sale on ebay and in 2011 it was bought by a Plym Valley Railway member for restoration and use on that line. ***Saturday 24th August 1963***

Scottish Gas Board, Provan Gas Works, Glasgow

Provan Gas Works was built by Glasgow Corporation at the very beginning of the twentieth century. It came under the Scottish Gas Board on nationalisation in 1948. When town gas production from coal ended with the introduction of natural gas in 1970 it continued in use for storage and distribution.

Two generations of Andrew Barclay products stood side by side for comparison at the Scottish Gas Board Provan Gas Works engine shed. No. 1, behind, was built in 1955 with the Works No. 2370. Its elder relative No. 3, like No. 1, was an outside cylinder 0-4-0 saddle tank but it dated from 1915 and had the Works No. 1425. ***Sunday 1st September 1963***

Scottish Gas Board No. 1 was a 14 x 22in. outside cylinder 0-4-0 saddle tank built in 1955 with the Works No. 2370 and delivered new to Proven Gas Works in Lanarkshire where it was photographed. It was the last Andrew Barclay industrial steam locomotive to be delivered in Scotland and it survived just into the next decade. ***Sunday 1st September 1963***

Scottish Gas Board No. 3 was originally delivered to the Glasgow Corporation Gas Department at Dawsholm Gas Works but was transferred to Provan Gas Works in April 1960 where it was at work here. It was scrapped around three years later. *Friday 16th April 1965*

No. 3 was a 16 x 24in. outside cylinder 0-4-0 saddle tank built by the North British Locomotive Co. at the Hyde Park Works, Glasgow, with the Works No. 19049 and delivered new to Provan Gas Works in 1911. It was clear from its rusty condition and with its coupling rods removed that it had been withdrawn from service several years earlier, presumably around the time the Andrew Barclay No. 3 arrived, when seen there but it was not scrapped until around four years later. *Sunday 1st September 1963*

Scottish Gas Board, Sandilands Gas Works, Aberdeen

The Aberdeen New Gas Light Company was formed in 1844 and erected its Sandilands Gas Works which was transferred to Aberdeen Town Council in 1871. The railway needed to transport coal from Aberdeen Docks came into use at the end of 1886. The gas works was nationalised and became part of the Scottish Gas Board on 1st May 1949 and later, in 1973, the British Gas Corporation. Coal gas manufacture ended and the works was demolished in 1975. In addition to the locomotives pictured, there were two more Barclay saddle tanks at the gas works at the time these photographs were taken and these were joined by two diesels during the following year. All three Barclays, and Black, Hawthorn *City of Aberdeen*, have been preserved. Barclay Works No. 807 built in 1897 is named *Bon Accord* and is at the Royal Deeside Railway and No. 3, Works No. 1889 built in 1926, is at the Grampian Transport Museum.

Scottish Gas Board *Mr Therm* ran in the street outside Aberdeen Gas Works with empty wagons on the way to collect coal at the docks. This locomotive is an 0-4-0 saddle tank with 12 x 20in. outside cylinders built by Andrew Barclay in 1947 with the Works No. 2239. The car is either a Standard 8 or 10 saloon, both of which had the same body shell. *Wednesday 28th August 1963*

Mr Therm had just crossed Regent Bridge at Aberdeen Victoria Dock. The bridge, built in 1904 where the Upper and Victoria Docks met, was a steel swing bridge operated by hydraulic power and it carried two railway tracks and road traffic. The bridge was dismantled in the 1970s as part of the redevelopment of Aberdeen Harbour to provide round the clock access for North Sea oil industry shipping. The clock tower of the flemish style neo-gothic granite (what else in the 'Granite City'?) Aberdeen New Town House can be seen behind the bridge. It was designed by Peddie and Kinnear and building started in 1868.

Scottish Gas Board Aberdeen Gas Works Andrew Barclay 0-4-0 saddle tank *Mr Therm* running in the street conveying coal from the docks to the gas works. *Wednesday 28th August 1963*

Mr Therm running alongside Aberdeen Victoria Dock. It was fitted with skirts over the pistons, rods and wheels as a safety measure for street working. *Mr Therm* was withdrawn from service when steam hauled railway traffic came to an end in 1964 and it was placed in Aberdeen's Seaton Park as part of a children's play area but was removed for cosmetic restoration in 2016 and returned painted in a bright red and yellow livery with steps up to one side of the cab and a slide to exit from the other. Not one for the purists! *Wednesday 28th August 1963*

The Aberdeen Gas Works locomen were proud of their locomotives as is witnessed by the clean condition. They kindly used *Mr Therm* to haul the venerable *City of Aberdeen* out of its shed so we could photograph it. *Wednesday 28th August 1963*

A shunter led the way as ***Mr Therm*** took its load of coal from the docks in Aberdeen to the gas works along Regent Quay past Craigmyle's newsagent and tobacconist. A Morris Minor Traveller completes the scene. This was the day that Martin Luther King Jr delivered his famous "***I Have a Dream***" speech at the Lincoln Memorial in Washington D.C.
Wednesday 28th August 1963

CRAIGMYLE
ROBERT DUTHIE & SONS LTD

City of Aberdeen was a rare *'Sassenach'* away from home. It was, and still is, a Black, Hawthorn Co. Ltd of Gateshead 12 x 18in. outside cylinder 0-4-0 saddle tank with the Works No. 912. It had relatively small 2ft 11in. driving wheels. It was delivered new to the Corporation of Aberdeen Gas Department in October 1887 and, like the other locomotives there, it was fitted with skirts for street working. Fortunately *City of Aberdeen* was donated by Scottish Gas to the Scottish Railway Preservation Society in 1977 and loaned to the Tanfield Railway. It is now at the Bo'ness and Kinneil Railway.

Scottish Malt Distillers Balmenach Distillery, Cromdale, Morayshire

Balmenach Distillery was linked to the ex-Great North of Scotland Railway at Cromdale by a one and a half mile long line which had opened in 1897. Cromdale station closed just two months after these photographs were taken and the Strathspey line closed to freight three years later. The Balmenach Distillery was established the year after the 1823 Excise Act permitting legal distilling was passed, though no doubt illicit *uisge beatha* had been produced there before.

Scottish Malt Distillers Balmenach Distillery at Cromdale employed a 12 x 20in. outside cylinder 0-4-0 saddle tank built by Andrew Barclay with the Works No. 2020. This was the sole locomotive at the site and it had replaced an Aveling & Porter 4wTG when delivered new in 1936. *Sunday 27th August 1965*

On the same day Scottish Malt Distillers Andrew Barclay Works No. 2020 ran light along the branch linking the distillery with the ex-Great North of Scotland line at Cromdale. In October 1968 the locomotive was transferred to Dailuaine Distillery, near Aberdour, and when withdrawn it was named *No 2 Balmenach* and placed on display not far from its original home at Boat of Garten on the Strathspey Railway. The area towards the hills behind, known as the Haughs of Cromdale, is the site of the routing of highland Jacobite forces by government troops on the last day of April 1690. It is the subject of a folk song and pipe tune. *Sunday 27th August 1965*

Mardy No 3, formerly War Department No. 186 ***Manipur Road***, and ex-Great Western Railway pannier tank No. 9792 working together to haul a heavy train at Mardy Colliery. *Wednesday 27th August 1969*

Part Three: Wales

Stratford-upon-Avon, my home town, was on the ex-Great Western Railway cross country main line from Wolverhampton Low Level and Birmingham Snow Hill to Cheltenham Malvern Road and Gloucester Eastgate or Central and continuing not only to Bristol and the West Country but also to Cardiff General, Swansea High Street and Carmarthen with through carriages all the way to Pembroke Dock on some services. Unfortunately these trains to South Wales were diverted onto the ex-Midland Railway line between Birmingham and Cheltenham, and so away from Stratford, in September 1962 but not before I and other local railway enthusiasts had taken advantage of them. During the 1959 summer school holiday a friend and I managed to get the ticket of our dreams: a Western Region Rail Rover. As we were only thirteen years old our mothers insisted we return home every evening so the convenient direct service to South Wales was a favourite. Apart from the obvious 'trainspotting' attraction of the main line sheds such as Cardiff Canton (86C), with its large home allocation including 'Castles' and 'Britannias' and visiting locomotives, there were other, initially unexpected, delights to be found particularly further along the line at Swansea East Dock (87D) and Danygraig (87C). Small, far less glamorous but much rarer, non standard industrial type 0-4-0 dock tanks were still in service. I saw ex-GWR Avonside Engine Co. built '1101' Class side tanks, ex-Cardiff Railway Kitson built saddle tank No. 1338 and a handful of former Powlesland and Mason and Swansea Harbour Trust Peckett, Hawthorn Leslie and Hudswell Clarke built saddle tanks that had entered GWR ownership. I soon discovered that there were Pecketts, Avonsides, Hudswell Clarkes and more in abundance in the Welsh Valleys from the informative Birmingham Locomotive Club Pocket Book 6: *Industrial Locomotives of South Wales and Monmouthshire* so on subsequent trips to South Wales in the early 1960s we set out to find a considerable number of interesting tank engines from a variety of builders. When an older friend had obtained his driving licence, a group of us occasionally hired a car for a day to visit the lines and sheds in the Welsh Valleys via the exciting and almost deserted new Ross Spur M50 motorway. I remember one of the cars was a black Austin A40 Farina. This gave us much more flexibility and as well as the valley sheds, with their collection of ex-GWR side and pannier tanks, we also visited industrial systems which were, of course, mainly at National Coal Board collieries. There was a surprise in store because we discovered a small number of second-hand pannier tanks that had originally been in service with the GWR. Two of them had even originated with pre-1923 grouping constituent companies. One of these was at a site that was not a colliery. *Dorothy*, built at Brush Electrical Engineering, Loughborough, was hiding in the

The last ex-British Railways standard gauge locomotive in non-preservation service was Great Western Railway-built No. 7754 at Mountain Ash Colliery.

bushes looking very abandoned along with a number of other locomotives at the Pontardawe Tinplate Works on Sunday 12th August 1962. Initially Powlesland and Mason No. 5 it became GWR No. 795 and was rebuilt as a pannier tank at Swindon Works. The second one was ex-Barry Railway J.H. Hosgood designed 'F' Class No. 138 which we found poking poking out of the engine shed at Hafodyrynys Colliery on Saturday 6th April 1963. Frustratingly, the narrow single road building meant it was impossible to get a side view photograph. We were just in time as both of these pannier tanks were only a few months away from being cut up. *Glendower*, a Hunslet Engine 0-6-0 saddle tank built in 1934, was also on site at Hafodyrynys as was an attractive unnamed Manning Wardle 0-6-0 saddle tank built in 1918. We also found two NCB light green liveried ex-GWR '2021' Class 0-6-0 pannier tanks on Saturday 6th April 1963. No. 2034 was inside the engine shed, with its coupling rods removed but cabside and smokebox number plates still attached, at Blaenavon Colliery. Sister engine No. 2092, which probably never worked again as its smokebox door handles were missing, was outside at Bargoed Colliery alongside several unusual Powell Duffryn pulverised coal hopper wagons built in the early 1940s as a wartime measure to convey compacted coal dust to Bargoed Power Station. It was fascinating to see a miners' train of ex-main-line vans very basically converted for passenger use on the NCB Talywain Railway and non-steam hay fuelled one-horsepower traction at work at Blaenavon Colliery. Another particularly interesting site was the Fairfield Shipbuilding and Engineering yard at Chepstow where two unusual locomotives were based. One, a Kerr Stuart well tank built in 1918, was of a type originally designed by James Cross about fifty years earlier for construction by E. Borrows and Sons' Providence Works at Sutton, near St. Helens. The other, ex-Great Eastern Railway '209' Class, later London and North Eastern Railway 'Y5' Class, No. 229, was an 'ogee' saddle tank built by Neilson & Co. in 1876. Fortunately both have been preserved.

In the north of the country the slate quarries, once the most productive in the world, were in serious decline. Two of the narrow gauge lines constructed to transport this heavy material, the Ffestiniog and the Talyllyn railways, were already running as popular tourist attractions but there were still locomotives at the quarries. At the time of my visits, a number of them were on the point of being sold and shipped to the United States and others were in a line of rusting hulks alongside the Penrhyn Quarries Coed-y-parc Works at Bethesda. Few people could have imagined then that all but one would now be preserved, many restored to working order, and the exported ones repatriated to Great Britain.

Industrial steam locomotives continued in use for a number of years after steam traction officially ended on British Railways and there was even a handful of ex-BR survivors to act as an antidote to main line withdrawal symptoms. By that time the engines often needed a little tender loving care and so sometimes before we photographed them in action a preliminary cleaning visit was planned. One example was No. 9792 at Mardy (or Maerdy in Welsh) Colliery at the end of March 1969 when, encouraged by photographer Mike Collins, the buffer beam was repainted and oily cotton waste used to polish up the paintwork as much as possible. It was surprising how little attention we attracted. We were obviously trespassing but were just allowed to get on with it. The one and a quarter mile long colliery line had a rural backdrop of the valley slopes which was good for photographs and one taken five months later shows No. 9792 looking very much like a BR locomotive with realistic replica cabside and smokebox numberplates and shedcode (88F - Treherbert) made by Mike in place. Sadly, despite all the polishing, unlike many other post BR survivors it was not preserved and it was scrapped in September 1973. I saw it working alongside *Mardy No. 3*, a Vulcan Foundry 0-6-0 saddle tank built in 1945 and rebuilt by Hunslet in 1961, and *Mardy No. 1*, a Peckett 'OQ' Class 0-6-0ST built in 1954. *Mardy No. 1* was not withdrawn from service until 1976 when it was sold for preservation. It is known as *Mardy Monster* because it has a tractive effort of 29,527, the highest, it is claimed, of any industrial steam locomotive in Britain.

No. 7754 was still in action early in the next decade at Mountain Ash on a snowy day in February 1971.

It is unsurprising considering its product that the National Coal Board retained a substantial fleet of different steam locomotive types from a number of manufacturers longer than many industrial sites which turned to diesel power. The very last ex-British Railways standard gauge steam locomotive in non-preservation activity was ex-Great Western Railway pannier tank No. 7754 which was not withdrawn until 1975. I was sent to Mountain Ash Comprehensive School as a trainee teacher in 1971 when No. 7754, along with other locomotives, was still very much in action at the local Deep Duffryn Colliery and visible busily about its duties through the classroom window. Bliss! Some friends thought I had somehow engineered this but it was just my good luck.

Chapter 13

National Coal Board Collieries in Gwent

Hafodyrynys Colliery

The ex-Crumlin Valley Collieries Ltd Hafodyrynys Colliery exchange sidings and washery were situated on the now closed ex-Great Western Vale of Neath line between Crumlin High Level and Pontypool Clarence Street stations. The colliery closed in 1966 though the, at the time, fairly modern washery continued in use by neighbouring collieries until early in 1978. The site was finally cleared in 1985.

Glendower, an 18 x 26in. inside cylinder Hunslet Engine Co. 0-6-0 saddle tank built in 1954 (Works No. 3810) in steam at Hafodyrynys Colliery. Delivered new to the National Coal Board Tirpentwys Colliery, Pontypool, it then moved on to the Talywain Railways in the summer of 1959 and was later transferred to Hafodyrynys. It may have worked for short periods at other collieries but it was withdrawn from Hafodyrynys in 1973 and went into preservation at the Avon Valley Railway at Bitton before moving to the Dart Valley Railway (now known as the South Devon Railway). *Saturday 6th April 1963*

ABOVE: An interesting find at NCB Hafodyrynys Colliery was ex-Barry Railway 'F' Class No. 138 in NCB green livery poking out of the engine shed. Frustratingly, the narrow single road building meant it was impossible to get a side view photograph. It was built by Hudswell, Clarke in 1905 as an 0-6-0 saddle tank with the Works No. 717 but it became Great Western Railway No. 780 at the grouping and was rebuilt with pannier tanks at Swindon in 1927. It was sold in May 1936 to Burnyeats Brown & Co. Ltd, Nine Mile Point Colliery, Gwent. After nationalisation it worked at a number of South Wales sites. Sadly it was scrapped at Hafodyrynys Colliery in May 1964.
Saturday 6th April 1963

LEFT: Manning, Wardle 0-6-0 saddle tank Works No. 1942 was seen in steam at Hafodyrynys Colliery. This 17 x 24in. outside cylinder 0-6-0 saddle tank was built in 1918 for the Inland Waterways & Docks Department, where it was No. 31. Surplus to requirements by 1922, it was sold to Partridge Jones & John Paton Ltd for use at Blaenserchan Colliery, part of the Talywain system, where it worked carrying the name *Blaenserchan*. It was rebuilt using parts from another Manning, Wardle locomotive around five years after nationalisation and was renamed *Syr Dafydd*. It stayed on the Talywain system, apart from a short stay at Tirpentwys Colliery, until transfer to Hafodyrynys Colliery in the early 1960s.
Monday 12th April 1965

Another look at the, by then nameless, Manning, Wardle 0-6-0 saddle tank 1942 at Hafodyrynys Colliery. It was transferred to the NCB Blaenavon railways five months after this picture was taken and it was scrapped in November 1968. *Monday 12th April 1965*

Gwent, a Hunslet Engine Co. 18 x 26in. inside cylinder 0-6-0 saddle tank built in 1952 (Works No. 3780), in action at Hafodyrynys Colliery. It was delivered new to the NCB Talywain Railways at Abersychan and then moved, via a short stay at Blaenavon Colliery, to Hafodyrynys Colliery in the Autumn of 1963. It was scrapped there in 1972. *Monday 12th April 1965*

British Railways, ex-Great Western Railway, '6100' Class 'Prairie' 2-6-2 side tank No. 6115 running past the impressive Hafodyrynys Colliery buildings at the head of a coal train on the now closed Pontypool Road to Aberdare High Level line. The Pontypool Road (86G) shedded locomotive was built at Swindon in 1931 and was withdrawn in November 1964.
Saturday 6th April 1963

Blaenavon Colliery

The ex-Blaenavon Colliery Company interchange with the main line was at Furness Sidings between Blaenavon High Level station and Garn-yr-Erw Halt on the ex-London & North Western Railway line to Brynmawr. This is now part of the preserved Pontypool & Blaenavon Railway. The main mine, Big Pit, was closed in 1980 but it has since become the Big Pit National Coal Museum which, along with the industrial heritage of the Blaenavon (Blaenafon in Welsh) area, has been named a World Heritage Site by UNESCO.

An ex-Great Western Railway '2021' Class 0-6-0 pannier tank, No. 2034, sitting inside the shed at NCB Blaenavon Colliery. It appeared to have already been taken out of service as its coupling rods had been removed but, interestingly, it still retained its smokebox and cabside number plates. It was built as a saddle tank at Wolverhampton Works in 1897 and later rebuilt as a pannier tank. It was withdrawn by British Railways in September 1955. It was then bought by the NCB for use at the Caerphilly Tar Distribution Plant but was later transferred to Hafodyrynys Colliery and then to Blaenavon where it was scrapped in March 1964. There is some doubt whether the class, as saddle tanks, was designed by George Armstrong or William Dean. *Saturday 6th April 1963*

I saw this one horsepower traction pulling narrow gauge 'trams' or 'tubs' at Blaenavon Colliery. Unfortunately I do not know the name or the age of the motive power! I have since learned, thanks to Ceri Thompson at the Big Pit National Coal Museum, that the driver was 'Nitch' Williams and that his job would probably have been termed 'surface hallier' (haulier). The smaller horse, or 'pit pony', in the picture left was called Bob and this is written, along with 'Big Pit', on his bonnet which has eye protection against flying debris. Wearing this probably means he had just come up to the surface or was about to go down. *Tuesday 2nd September 1969*

Celynen North Colliery

The ex-Partridge, Jones & John Paton colliery was situated between Newbridge and Crumlin Low Level stations on the ex-Great Western Railway to Ebbw Vale. Passenger services on this line ceased in 1962 but the line remained open for freight, particularly to the Ebbw Vale steelworks, until 2002 which protected the infrastructure and has enabled restoration of passenger services. A diesel shunter arrived at Celynen North in 1971 replacing steam traction there until rail traffic came to an end in 1979 when it was linked to Oakdale Colliery where the coal was then lifted. Both collieries closed in 1989.

Celynen North Colliery was situated in the Ebbw Valley. There was a junction linking the colliery sidings with British Railways line at the bottom of the incline near Crumlin Low Level station. Celynen North Halt was out of sight, at a lower level, just to the left of this photograph.The impressive Crumlin Viaduct crossing the valley, which was the highest in Great Britain, dominated the scene. This was built as part of the Taff Vale Extension Railway linking Aberdare to Pontypool and it was officially opened in 1857. After closure of the line the iron parts of the viaduct were all dismantled by the end of 1967 but before that it was used in scenes for the 1966 film *Arabesque* starring Sophia Loren and Gregory Peck. *Monday 12th April 1965*

Joan No. 12A, a 14 x 22in. outside cylinder 0-4-0 saddle tank built by Andrew Barclay in 1905 (Works No. 1011), at work at Celynen North Colliery. This locomotive was delivered new to the Swansea Harbour Trust in 1905 as their No. 4 but was sold to the Blaenavon Co. Ltd in 1915. This was only eight years before the SHT, along with its locomotive fleet, was absorbed into the Great Western Railway. It remained on the Blaenavon Railways, apart from a short stay at Six Bells Colliery, until it was transferred to Celynen North Colliery at Newbridge in January 1964. Overlooking the scene is the unusual Italian style St. Mary of Peace Catholic church. *Monday 12th April 1965*

Another look at ***Joan No. 12A*** hard at work at Celynen North Colliery. It returned to Blaenavon at the beginning of 1966 and was scrapped in the second half of 1967. *Monday 12th April 1965*

Looking the worse for wear, Hawthorn, Leslie 16 x 24in. outside cylinder 0-6-0 saddle tank No. 58 at work at Celynen North Colliery. It was built in 1937 (Works No. 3923) and delivered new to the Richard Thomas and Baldwins Ltd Ebbw Vale Works. It had arrived at Celynen North early in 1962 but was transferred to Celynen South Colliery the year after this photograph was taken and scrapped there in 1975. *Friday 25th September 1970*

Blaenserchan Colliery and the Talywain Railway

Blaenserchan Colliery was sunk by Partridge Jones & Co. Ltd in 1890. Along with the other coal mines in Britain, it became part of the National Coal Board on nationalisation on 1st January 1947. The pit finally closed on 8th August 1985. The Talywain Railway ran for about two and a half miles between the colliery and a connection with the ex-Great Western Railway line near Abersychan & Talywain station.

On New Year's Eve 1968, ***Illtyd***, an Andrew Barclay Sons and Company of Kilmarnock 17 x 24in. outside cylinder 0-6-0 saddle tank locomotive built in 1952 (Works No. 2331), was hard at work on the NCB Talywain system (Talywaun in Welsh). *Tuesday 31st December 1968*

Illtyd is seen again on the NCB Talywain system on New Year's Eve 1968. It was based at the NCB engine depot at Talywain for its entire working life until it was scrapped there in April 1975. Illtyd was a Welsh saint who was born in Armorica (Brittany) in the late 5th century and there is a hamlet called St. Illtyd near Aberbeeg. *Tuesday 31st December 1968*

Illtyd on a cross-country run returning with a train of empty wagons to Blaenserchan Colliery on the Talywain system. *Tuesday 2nd September 1969*

Llewellyn was seen on the climb approaching Ty-Rhiw Frank level crossing on the NCB Talywain system going towards Blaenserchan on a train of four ex-GWR 'Mink' vans and one ex-LM&SR van on New Year's Eve 1968. These vans had been adapted for use as carriages for the miners at that time on what was sometimes called a 'Paddy Train' but not, I believe, there. The terraced houses in the British village, of which only the Eastview Cottage terrace in British Road still exists, and the Cwm Byrgwm slag tip can be seen in the middle distance. ***Llewellyn*** was a Hunslet 18 x 26in. inside cylinder 'Austerity' Type 0-6-0 saddle tank built in 1954 (Works No. 3817). It had been delivered new to NCB Talywain. It was transferred to Hafodyrynys Colliery sometime before May 1972 where it survived until it was cut up during the summer of 1976. *Tuesday 31st December 1968*

Chapter 14

National Coal Board Collieries in Glamorgan

Bargoed Colliery

The Powell Duffryn Steam Coal Co. Ltd Bargoed Colliery was sunk in 1897. It was in the Rhymney Valley just on the Montgomeryshire side of the border with Glamorgan between the now closed ex-Brecon & Merthyr Junction Railway and the ex-Rhymney Railway lines and it had rail connection with both. A number of diesel shunters, including some on hire from BR, worked there after the end of steam. The colliery washery closed in 1981 though coal extraction had ended several years earlier.

No. 16 was a 17 x 24in. inside cylinder Hudswell, Clarke 0-6-0 saddle tank built at the factory in Leeds in 1913 (Works No. 1012). It was seen dumped out of action at the end of a siding at Bargoed Colliery. It had been transferred to Bargoed from Penallta Colliery in 1960 but had worked at Bargoed before. Both collieries belonged to Powell Duffryn Ltd prior to nationalisation in 1947. No. 16 was cut up in the spring of 1965. *Saturday 6th April 1963*

Ex-Great Western Railway '2021' Class 0-6-0 pannier tank No. 2092 standing out of steam at Bargoed Colliery. It probably never worked again as its smokebox door handles were missing. It had been built as one of a class of 140 saddle tanks at Wolverhampton Works in 1901. All of the '2021' Class were later rebuilt as pannier tanks and after withdrawal by British Railways in August 1955 No. 2092 was bought by the NCB early the following year for use at Bargoed. Some unusual Powell Duffryn pulverised coal hopper wagons can be seen behind the locomotive. These were built in the 1940s as a wartime measure to convey compacted coal dust to Bargoed Power Station. *Saturday 6th April 1963*

A second look at ex-GWR '2021' Class 0-6-0 pannier tank No. 2092 out of action, probably for ever, at Bargoed Colliery. Apart from a very short stay at Groesfaen Colliery, it spent all its National Coal Board working life at Bargoed Colliery until it was finally scrapped in the second half of 1964. Note the aerial ropeway overhead. ***Saturday 6th April 1963***

Deep Navigation Colliery

The ex-Ocean & United National Collieries Ltd colliery at Treharris produced coal from 1879. In 1893 it was named Ocean Colliery to promote its production of good quality steam coal supplied, among others, to Cunard liners. It was renamed Deep Navigation Colliery after it was nationalised in 1947. After the demise of the NCB in 1987, it continued in operation under the control of the privatised British Coal but production ceased in March 1991. The site, along with two neighbouring collieries, has become the landscaped Parc Taf Bargoed.

Ferndale, **a 14 x 22in. outside cylinder Hawthorn, Leslie & Co. 0-6-0 saddle tank built in 1915 (Works No. 3133), standing in front of the engine shed at Deep Navigation Colliery. It had obviously received a bad knock to its cylinder casing. It had been delivered new to the Welsh Navigation Steam Coal Co. Ltd Coed Ely Colliery at Tonyrefail. It later moved to Mardy Colliery and then, in 1955, to Taff Merthyr Colliery and in the following year to Deep Navigation Colliery, both at Treharris. It was cut up in April 1966.**
Saturday 6th April 1963

Mardy Colliery

The ex-Powell Duffryn Mardy Colliery (Maerdy in Welsh) was situated between the village of Maerdy and Castell Nos Reservoir in the upper Rhondda Fach Valley. This colliery had a chequered history because it was closed in 1935 and then re-opened in 1938 but closed again in 1940 since coal could not be exported at that time. It was reopened again by the National Coal Board in 1949 with a large investment to modernise it. It was connected to the ex-Taff Vale Railway at Maerdy station by a one and a quarter mile branch. The station was the terminus for British Railways passenger trains until these were withdrawn in 1964 leaving the line solely in use by colliery trains until it became redundant in August 1986 after Mardy Colliery coal was raised at the connected Tower Colliery. It is now a cycle way. The colliery finally closed in December 1990.

Ex-GWR 0-6-0 pannier tank No. 9792 got some pre-photograph TLC at the Mardy Colliery locomotive shed. White trousers were probably inadvisable! No. 9792 was built at Swindon in 1936 and when withdrawn by British Railways, from Neath Court Sart shed (87A) in 1964, it went to the NCB Aberaman Railways but was transferred to Mardy Colliery the following year. *Sunday 30th March 1969*

After some polish and paint at Mardy Colliery, No. 9792 sported a replica smokebox number plate. It seems it had spent all its British Railways working life at Neath Court Sart shed (87A). Vulcan Foundry 0-6-0 saddle tank *Mardy No 3* was alongside.
Sunday 30th March 1969

Some of the polish had disappeared under the grime when No. 9792 was on duty five months later. It was seen with *Mardy No 3* in the background on the one and a quarter mile long line at Mardy Colliery. It seems it was given the name *Mardy No 4* and this had been painted roughly in small letters on the cabside, along with the No. 9792, where the original GWR number plate should have been.
Wednesday 27th August 1969

A little later that day, No. 9792 was carrying authentic looking replica cabside and smokebox number plates and an 88F (Treherbert) shed-plate prepared by Mike Collins. *Wednesday 27th August 1969*

A disguised No. 9792 sporting its replica number plate looked convincingly like a British Railways era locomotive at Mardy. Sadly, unlike many other post BR survivors, it was not preserved and it was scrapped in September 1973. *Wednesday 27th August 1969*

Mardy No. 1 steaming in the Winter sunshine with a rake of internal use wagons behind at Mardy Colliery in the Rhondda Valley. It is a Peckett 'OQ' Type 18 x 26in. outside cylinder 0-6-0 saddle tank with Stephenson inside valve gear built in 1954 (Works No. 2150). It has large 4ft0½in. driving wheels. This 'OQ' was originally designed for heavy work at the Port Talbot steelworks, at that time belonging to the Steel Company of Wales, but it was sold to the National Coal Board instead.
Monday 30th December 1968

Another look at *Mardy No. 1* at Mardy Colliery. It was withdrawn from service in 1976 and a few years later went into preservation on the Swanage Railway where it was not used so it was moved on to the Elsecar Heritage Railway, near Barnsley, and restored to steam. It has worked on loan at the East Lancashire Railway and the Lincolnshire Wolds Railway and was recently offered for sale. It has been given the nickname *Mardy Monster* because it has a tractive effort of 29,527, the highest, it is claimed, of any industrial steam locomotive in Britain.
Monday 30th December 1968

Mardy No. 3 in steam at Mardy Colliery. This was a Vulcan Foundry 18 x 26in. inside cylinder Hunslet 'Austerity' Type 0-6-0 saddle tank built in 1945 (Works No. 5280). It was originally a War Department locomotive numbered 75290, and later WD No. 186. It was named *Manipur Road*, after a Second World War military base in India, and it worked at several sites including the Marchwood Military Railway, near Southampton, and the Longmoor Military Railway. When no longer required by the military, it was rebuilt by Hunslet, in 1961, and became a National Coal Board engine at Mardy.
Monday 30th December 1968

Mardy No. 3 hard at work at Mardy Colliery in the Rhondda Valley. It was cut up by a Newport scrap merchant in 1973. *Wednesday 27th August 1969*

I was surprised to see ex-L&NER 'J94' Class No. 68070, on its way to a new owner in South Wales, and ex-Somerset & Dorset Joint Railway '7F' 2-8-0 No. 53807 together among the more usual residents on Gloucester Barnwood shed (85C) in April 1963. No. 53807 (ex-S&DJR No. 87) still had eighteen months of service left and had probably been sent here to have its wheelsets attended to, Barnwood having a covered wheeldrop facility which was regularly used by S&D line engines shedded at Bath Green Park. The 0-6-0ST was built for the War Department as WD No. 71486 by Robert Stephenson & Hawthorns in 1945 (Works No. 7295). It became L&NER No. 8070 in June 1946 when it was one of seventy-five of the type bought by the L&NER and classified 'J94'. Withdrawn in March 1963, from Mexborough shed (36B), it was sold to the National Coal Board and used at the Glyn Neath Disposal Point where, when no longer required, it was scrapped by Cashmore's in 1969. Coincidentally, the '7F' was also built by Robert Stephenson & Hawthorns, in 1925. *April 1963*

Aberaman Works

The ex-Powell Duffryn Aberaman Workshops served the Aberaman Railway which was made up of several branches linking a number of collieries to the west of the main connection with British Railways which was just to the south of the now closed Aberaman station on the ex-Taff Vale line from Pontypridd to Aberdare.

No. 1 inside the NCB Aberaman Works. This was an Andrew Barclay 18 x 24in. outside cylinder 0-6-0 side tank built in 1953, Works No. 2340. It had been delivered new to the NCB Aberaman Railways and was transferred to Merthyr Vale Colliery in October 1965. *Saturday 6th April 1963*

Merthyr Vale Colliery

The ex-Powell Duffryn Steam Coal Co. Merthyr Vale Colliery produced coal from 1875. The connection with British Railways was at Black Lion Loop, where there was a signal box and there had been a halt until 1924, not far from Merthyr Vale station on the still open ex-Taff Vale line to Merthyr Tydfil. The colliery continued to use a number of ex-British Railways diesel shunters after steam was withdrawn. It closed on 25th August 1989 and the site is being redeveloped under the title 'Project Riverside' to include homes, a school, shops and offices. Merthyr Vale is sadly noted for the Aberfan Disaster on 21st October 1966 when part of a large tip of waste on the opposite side of the River Taff to the colliery broke away and tons of spoil in the form of slurry slid into the village engulfing homes and a school.

More than five and a half years after it was photographed in Aberaman Works the Andrew Barclay No. 1 was in action overlooking the Afon Taff at Merthyr Vale Colliery. It had been transferred to Merthyr Vale in 1965 and, apart from a short period at Mardy from 1966 to 1967, it remained there until it was cut up at the end of summer in 1975. *Monday 30th December 1968*

Another view of No. 1, Andrew Barclay Works No. 2340, at Merthyr Vale Colliery. It was running along the half viaduct, half retaining wall construction by the Afon Taff built to connect the colliery with the ex-Taff Vale Railway Merthyr Tydfil to Cardiff line alongside. *Monday 30th December 1968*

The Andrew Barclay side tank No. 1 running past the houses in Taff Street by the Afon Taff at Merthyr Vale. These houses have since been condemned to be demolished because of the risk of flooding. The railway in the foreground is the Merthyr Tydfil to Cardiff line. *Wednesday 27th August 1969*

No. 1 was still at work at NCB Merthyr Vale on Wednesday 21st October 1970. The now demolished houses in Brynteg Terrace on Cardiff Road are behind and the ex-Taff Vale Railway line from Merthyr Tydfil to Cardiff ran between the colliery line and the buildings above. *Wednesday 21st October 1970*

Ex-Great Western Railway 0-6-0 pannier tank No. 9600 in steam at Merthyr Vale Colliery. Despite its clean BR appearance with number plates and lion and wheel totem on the tank side, this was almost three years after the last use of regular standard gauge steam on the Western Region and four months after the famous 'Fifteen Guinea Special', marking the end of its use on any British Railways region. No. 9600 had been sold to the NCB in October 1965 after it was withdrawn from BR service at Newport Ebbw Junction shed (86B). *Monday 30th December 1968*

No. 9600 working hard at Merthyr Vale Colliery during the morning. When this 1945 Swindon built locomotive was withdrawn in turn by the NCB, in 1973, it was bought for preservation and is now to be found at the Standard Gauge Steam Trust at the Tyseley Locomotive Works in Birmingham. Aberfan is on the other side of the River Taff. This was the site of the terrible disaster caused by the slipping of the Merthyr Vale slag heaps on 21st October 1966. *Monday 30th December 1968*

Mountain Ash Railways

The ex-Powell Duffryn Ltd Mountain Ash Railways served Deep Duffryn Washery and Deep Duffryn, Abergorki, and Cwm Cynon collieries. The shed and Mountain Ash Central Workshops were situated at Abergorki. There were connections with British Railways at the ex-Vale of Neath Railway Cardiff Road station and at the parallel ex-Taff Vale line on the opposite side of the Afon Cynon. The Aberaman Phurnicite Plant, which had previously been linked to the Aberaman Railways, was added in 1971, made possible by using two miles of the by then closed BR Vale of Neath line, as was, in 1972, Penrikyber (Penrhiwceiber) Colliery via an aerial conveyer. Deep Duffryn Colliery was later considered to be uneconomic and this lead to its closure in 1979 with the washery following the next year. Mountain Ash Railways continued to serve the Phurnicite Plant until 1981 leaving just the Central Workshops active for four more years.

The venerable No. 3, a Fox, Walker & Sons outside cylinder 0-6-0 saddle tank (Works No. 242), looked as if it had an uncertain future at Mountain Ash. It was delivered new to Nixon, Taylor and Cory Collieries' Mountain Ash System in 1874 and remained there when it became Powell Duffryn Ltd and, later, part of the National Coal Board until it was moved for preservation five months after this photograph was taken. Its present home is very appropriately in Bristol, the town where the Fox, Walker & Sons, later Peckett & Sons, Atlas Engine Works was sited. *Saturday 6th April 1963*

No. 8, an 18 x 26in. inside cylinder 0-6-0 saddle tank built by Robert Stephenson & Hawthorns Ltd in 1944 (Works No. 7139), seen passing under the B4275 road bridge at Mountain Ash. This was a wartime 'Austerity' Type locomotive and was originally War Department No. 75189 at the Longmoor Military Railway and later WD No. 152 with the name *Rennes*. It was rebuilt by Hunslet in 1961 before going to Mountain Ash. In 1982 it went to the Blaenavon Steam Trust at the Big Pit Museum for preservation and later to the Dean Forest Railway where it has been restored in the Longmoor Railway blue livery. *Wednesday 27th August 1969*

Seen here from the vantage point of the B4275 road bridge is No. 7754 crossing the Afon Cynon at Mountain Ash. The church is St. Margaret's in Dyffryn Road. No. 7754 was built for the GWR by the North British Locomotive Company in 1930 (Works No. 24042) and was withdrawn by British Railways from Wellington shed (84H) and sold to the NCB for use at Windsor Colliery in 1959. After moves to Llanbradach, Ogilvie, Elliot and Talywain, it had been transferred to Mountain Ash five months before this photograph was taken. *Wednesday 21st October 1970*

A general view of Mountain Ash Deep Duffryn Colliery seen from the B4275 road bridge with No. 7754 visible in the distance shunting well filled mineral wagons. It continued to work for around five more years and became the last of the class, some of which remained in service on the London Underground until 1971, to be in use other than in preservation. It can lay claim to having been the very last ex-BR standard gauge locomotive in regular non-preserved service. *Wednesday 21st October 1970*

Looking in the opposite direction from the B4275 road bridge, No. 7754 is running alongside the Afon Cynon at Mountain Ash. The site of the by then closed and abandoned British Railways Cardiff Road station can be seen just to the left behind the locomotive and the colliery engine shed is in the distance to the right with the Abergorki Colliery winding gear beyond. *Wednesday 21st October 1970*

In better times for Mountain Ash Cardiff Road station, British Railways ex-GWR Pontypool Road (86G) allocated 0-6-0 pannier tank No. 3708 pulled away towards Aberdare past the now demolished Allen's Arms hotel on a local passenger train. Originally the Vale of Neath Railway, this ex-Great Western line is now closed and lifted and this is the site of a present day car park. The lines to the right ran to the colliery. There was also a Taff Vale line Oxford Street station separated from the GWR one by the Afon Cynon. Saturday 6th April 1963

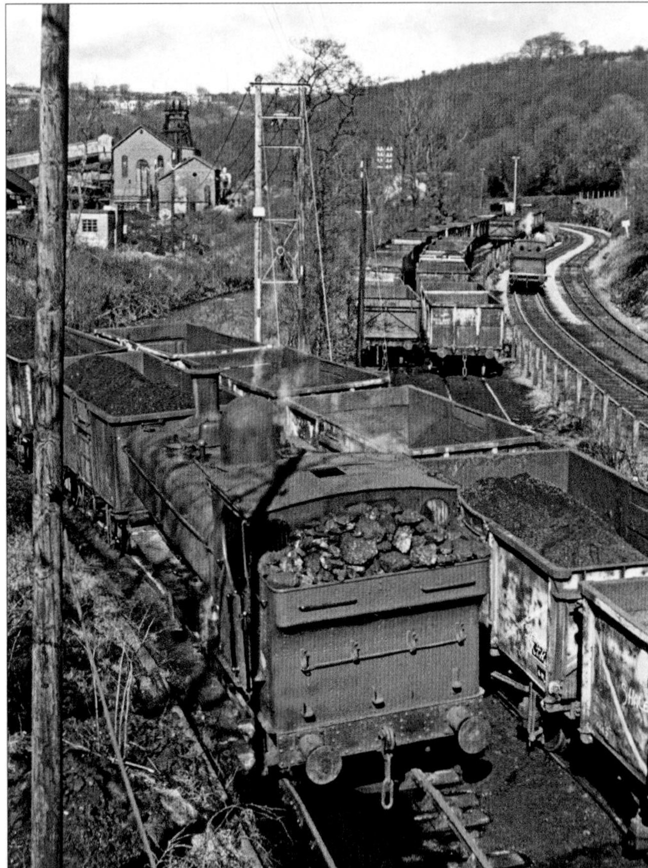

No. 7754 was still at work at Mountain Ash early in 1971. The Avonside Engine Co. ***Sir John*** can be seen in the distance on the right along the line that ran to the Aberaman Phurnacite Plant. Apparently, after No. 7754 was taken out of service, it was stored in the colliery engine shed until 1980 when it was presented by the NCB to the National Museum of Wales and placed on loan at the Llangollen Railway. It is now owned by the Llangollen Railway Trust.

Sir John taking a truck across the Afon Cynon at Mountain Ash. This is an Avonside Engine Co. 14 x 20 in. outside cylinder 'B3' Type 0-6-0 saddle tank built in 1914 with the Works No. 1680. *Friday 25th September 1970*

Another look at ***Sir John*** as it approached the junction with the line to the Aberaman Phurnacite Plant on the right at Mountain Ash that day. It was built as part of a War Department order and was based at Tidworth Camp in Hampshire until it was serviced by Avonside in 1929 and sold via the dealer George Cohen to Llewllyn (Nixon) Ltd, Mountain Ash Colliery the same year. *Friday 25th September 1970*

Sir John was in action again at Mountain Ash early in 1971. It was sold for preservation to the Taff Vale Railway Preservation Society in 1981 and then it passed on to the Vale of Neath Railway in 1987. It is now in store at the Pontypool and Blaenavon Railway.

This Kerr, Stuart & Co. 14½ x 20in. outside cylinder 0-4-0 well tank was built in 1918 with the Works No. 3063. It was delivered new to the National Shipyard No. 2 at Beachley but was soon transferred to the nearby National Shipyard No. 1 at Chepstow. By the mid-1970s this unusual locomotive was definitely out of use and starting to disappear in the undergrowth but fortunately it was bought and moved first to the Swindon and Cricklade Railway, in 1982, and later to the Flour Mill Works at Bream in the Forest of Dean for restoration. It was returned to steam in 2012 and is still based there although it has visited the Avon Valley, Chasewater and Foxfield railways. It has been given the name *Willy. Monday 12th April 1965*

Although Kerr Stuart & Co. Works No. 3063 was built in 1918 the type was originally designed by James Cross about fifty years earlier for construction by E. Borrows & Sons' Providence Works at Sutton, near St. Helens in, at the time, Lancashire. It is seen here still at Fairfield Engineering & Shipbuilding in Chepstow. The black plate showing that it was registered to run onto British Railways lines by the British Transport Commission as No. 1865 in 1953 can be seen on the cabside. *Saturday 31st July 1965*

Chapter 15

Welsh Industry

Fairfield Shipbuilding & Engineering, Chepstow, Monmouthshire

National Shipyard No. 1 at Chepstow was developed from an earlier yard by the River Wye which was taken over by the Ministry of Shipping in 1917, during the First World War. It was acquired by the Monmouth Shipbuilding Co. Ltd after the end of hostilities and then by Fairfield Shipbuilding & Engineering in 1926 and remained with that company until the year after these photographs were taken when it became Fairfield-Mabey Ltd which specialises in steel bridge construction. There was a rail connection with the Great Western Railway main line at Chepstow and two diesel mechanical and two diesel hydraulic shunting locomotives were used after the end of steam. Rail traffic finally ended in 1985.

Ex-Great Eastern Railway '209' Class No. 229, later renumbered 0229, is a 12 x 18in. outside cylinder 0-4-0 'ogee' saddle tank built by Neilson & Co. in 1876 with the Works No. 2119. It was sold to the Admiralty in 1917 to work at the National Shipyard No. 1 at Chepstow. It was still at the, by then, Fairfield Shipbuilding & Engineering yard at Chepstow on Saturday 31st July 1965 but it had clearly been out of use for a while. This last example of the eight built of the type, which later became London & North Eastern Railway 'Y5' Class , was bought for preservation and it first went to the now closed North Woolwich Station Museum and subsequently, in November 1982, to the Flour Mill Works at Bream in the Forest of Dean. *Saturday 31st July 1965*

Bird's Scrapyard at Pontymister, Gwent

Partridge, Jones & John Paton Ltd acquired the Monmouthshire Steel & Tinplate Co. Ltd Pontymister Works, which dated from 1801, in 1920. After production ended in January 1962, the works were demolished by Bird's Commercial Motors Ltd and the site was then used by them as a scrapyard.

Upper Boat, a Hawthorn, Leslie 14 x 22in. outside cylinder 0-4-0 saddle tank built in 1936 with the Works No. 3877, originally worked at the Central Electricity Generating Board Llynfi Generating Station near Bridgend but it had arrived at Bird's scrapyard at Pontymister some time before this photograph was taken. It was used for a while at this site to help in the clearance of the former Pontymister Steelworks which was where many ex BR locomotives were then scrapped. *Upper Boat* joined them in this fate and it was cut up early in 1964. What appears to be a Metropolitan Line 'F' stock steel underground train, all of which were all taken out of service by the spring of 1963, is behind. *Saturday 6th April 1963*

Richard Thomas & Baldwins Ltd, Pontardawe Tinplate Works, West Glamorgan

Richard Thomas & Baldwins Ltd Pontardawe Tinplate Works, which had earlier belonged to W. Gilbertson & Company, finally closed at the end of August 1962. After demolition Cwmtawe Comprehensive School, Pontardawe Leisure Centre and stores in the Pontardawe Retail Park were constructed on the site.

Finedon standing outside the engine shed at the Pontardawe Tinplate Works. This was just days before the works closed on 31st August. *Finedon* was an Andrew Barclay 14 x 22in. outside cylinder 0-4-0 saddle tank built in 1941 (Works No. 2129) which had been delivered new to the Finedon Ironstone Quarries in Northamptonshire. It arrived at Pontardawe in 1946 and it was scrapped at the end of 1963. *Sunday 12th August 1962*

Catching a rare shaft of sunlight, No. 7 ***Beaufort***, a Peckett 'E' Type 0-4-0 saddle tank with 15 x 21in. outside cylinders and 3ft 7in. wheels, was also at the Pontardawe Tinplate Works that day. It was built in 1903 with the Works No. 1011 and it had come to Pontardawe from the Richard Thomas & Baldwins Ltd Duffryn Works in Morriston six months before this photograph was taken. It had previously worked at Cwmfelin Steel & Tinplate Works, near Swansea, and before that at the Ebbw Vale Works at Newport where it had gone when new. It was scrapped at the end of 1963. *Sunday 12th August 1962*

James Watt, another Peckett 'E' Type 15 x 21in. outside cylinder 0-4-0 saddle tank, had a similar history to its sister ***Beaufort***. Built in 1904 (Works No. 1013), it was also delivered new to the Ebbw Vale Works at Newport but it was transferred directly to the Pontardawe Tinplate Works in 1955. It appeared to be out of use there when photographed and it was scrapped at the end of 1963. The wagon has the instruction 'Not to be used for P R ballast or other engineering materials' on it. *Sunday 12th August 1962*

Lucy looking abandoned but shiny in the shrubbery after a downpour at Pontardawe Tinplate Works. This 14 x 20in. outside cylinder 0-4-0 saddle tank was built by Hudswell, Clarke in 1920 (Works No. 1401). It had originally worked at the Highley Mineral Company Kinlet Colliery in Shropshire (connected to the now preserved Severn Valley Railway) but moved to Pontardawe in 1939. It was scrapped during the summer of 1963. *Sunday 12th August 1962*

Dorothy was spotted hiding in the bushes at Pontardawe Tinplate Works on the same day. It was built as a saddle tank by Brush Electrical Engineering at Loughborough in 1903 with the Works No. 301 for Powlesland & Mason as their No. 5 for use at Swansea Docks. It became Great Western Railway No. 795 at the grouping in 1923 and, in 1926, it was rebuilt as a pannier tank at Swindon Works. It was then sold to what was at the time W. Gilbertson & Co. Pontardawe Steel and Tinplate Works in 1929. It had 14 x 20in. outside cylinders. Sadly this unusual locomotive was scrapped later in the year the photograph was taken. *Sunday 12th August 1962*

British Steel Corporation, Abercarn Works, Gwent

The ex-Richard Thomas & Baldwins Ltd Abercarn Works was host to only one steam locomotive along with a John Fowler diesel mechanical shunter at the time these photographs were taken. The rail connection was by the now closed Abercarn station on the ex-Great Western Railway in the Ebbw Valley. The works closed in 1981.

Andrew Barclay 12 x 20in. outside cylinder 0-4-0 saddle tank *Forester,* built in 1911 (Works No. 1260), at the Abercarn Works. It had been supplied new to the, at the time, Newport Tinplate Co. Ltd Abercarn Works and it stayed there while the company ownership changed to Richard Thomas & Co. Ltd and then Richard Thomas & Baldwins Ltd which was absorbed into the British Steel Corporation in 1968. *Tuesday 2nd September 1969*

Another look at *Forester* at Abercarn Tinplate Works. When surplus to requirements in 1970, shortly after this photograph was taken, *Forester* was transferred to the Ebbw Vale Works for preservation. It was then placed on static display on the site of the old Blaenavon Wharf alongside the River Usk in Newport where it was unfortunately the subject of vandalism until the council donated it to the Pontypool & Blaenavon Railway Society at the Big Pit Mining Museum at Blaenavon and it was moved there in November 2012. *Tuesday 2nd September 1969*

Guest, Keen & Nettlefolds Brymbo Steelworks, Denbighshire

The Guest, Keen & Nettlefolds Brymbo Steelworks near Wrexham, on a site where iron had been produced since about 1796, was nationalised and became part of the British Steel Corporation in 1967.

It finally closed with the loss of many jobs in 1990 by which time it was owned by United Engineering Steels. Rail connection was with the Wrexham and Minera Branch of the Great Western Railway.

Anzac, in its distinctive yellow livery, visible from the road at the Brymbo Steelworks. This 16 x 24in. outside cylinder 0-6-0 saddle tank was a Hawthorn, Leslie product built in 1916 with the Works No. 3214. It was delivered to the Brymbo Steel Co. Ltd in January 1917 and remained there until it was scrapped early in 1965. *Anzac* was one of only three steam locomotives remaining at Brymbo at the time. The other two, Robert Stephenson and Hawthorns *Sir Henry* and Peckett 'B3' *Berwyn*, both 0-6-0 saddle tanks, were scrapped early in 1966 leaving a large fleet of Yorkshire Engine Co. Ltd diesel-electric locomotives in charge of traffic. *Monday 11th June 1962*

Chapter 16
Narrow Gauge
The North Wales Slate Quarries

Welsh slate was, and to a much lesser extent still is, used throughout Britain and exported all over the world, particularly for roofing but also for other purposes. The quarries were situated inland so rail transport to the transshipment points, either the main-line railway or ports, was obviously essential for this very heavy material. This was the reason for the construction of several of the now preserved heritage narrow gauge lines that are in operation in Wales such as the Ffestiniog and Talyllyn railways. Dinorwic and Penrhyn were the two largest slate quarries in the world and they, as did others, also used rail transport in the galleries within their workings.

Dorothea Slate Quarries, Nantlle

Slate was taken from Dorothea Quarries on the horse-drawn 3ft 6in. gauge Nantlle Tramway to the exchange sidings at Nantlle where it was loaded onto standard gauge wagons to continue to Caernarfon on the the ex-London & North Western Railway branch. The internal quarry rail system was 2ft 0in. gauge and there were two steam locomotives, both of which were taken out of service during the 1940s. After nearly twenty years out of use they were bought for preservation and both have been restored to working order. They are *Dorothea*, a Hunslet saddle tank built in 1901 which is now at the Launceston Steam Railway, and *Wendy*. The quarry closed in 1970.

Wendy, a 2ft gauge W.G. Bagnall outside cylinder 0-4-0 saddle tank built in 1919 with the Works No. 2091 for the Ministry of Munitions, at Dorothea Slate Quarries. As it was not completed until after the end of the First World War it was surplus to requirements and sold to the Votty & Bowydd slate quarry at Blaenau Ffestiniog. In 1930 it was bought by the Dorothea Slate Quarry Co. but it was taken out of service with a fractured steam pipe in the mid 1940s and remained rusting away until around the time this photograph was taken when it was bought by the Hampshire Narrow Gauge Society. *Wendy* was rebuilt and restored as much as possible to its original condition but it was not until 1979 that it moved under its own power for the first time. It was based at the Bursledon Brickworks Museum until that closed and it was moved to the Statfold Barn Railway. It has worked on the Amberly Chalk Pits line and on the Hayling Seaside Railway. *Sunday 10th June 1962*

Dinorwic Quarries, Llanberis

The Dinorwic slate quarries were linked to Port Dinorwic (Y Felinheli in Welsh) by the seven-mile long Padarn Railway which was laid to the unusual four foot gauge and was closed in November 1961. The quarry locomotives were 1ft 10¾in. gauge. I recall that *Fire Queen*, a 4ft gauge locomotive built by A. Horlock and Co. in 1848 and taken out of service well before the end of the 19th century, was inside a small shed when I visited in 1962. Fortunately, unlike the later locomotives of the same gauge, it has survived and is now at the Penrhyn Castle Museum. The quarry closed in July 1969. Part of the Padarn Railway has been relaid to 1ft 11½in. gauge and reopened as the Llanberis Lake Railway and the Dinorwic workshops have become the National Slate Museum.

Dinorwic sheltered out of use at the Dinorwic Quarry, Llanberis eight months after the line had closed. This locomotive was a Hunslet Engine Co. 4ft gauge, 12½ x 20in. outside cylinder 0-6-0 side tank built in 1882 with the Works No. 302 and it was the oldest of three Hunslet side tanks which had worked there. It was scrapped in 1963. _Sunday 10th June 1962_

Cackler inside the Dinorwic Gilfach Ddu Workshops at Llanberis. It was one of two 'Mills' Class $8^1/_2$x 14in. outside cylinder 1 ft $10^3/_4$in. gauge 0-4-0 saddle tank locomotives delivered to Dinorwic by the Hunslet Engine Co. It was built in 1898 with the Works No. 671 and was originally named _Port Dinorwic_. A number of Dinorwic locomotives were named after racehorses and so it became _Cackler_ after the twice winner of the Grand Sefton Steeplechase in 1909 and 1910. It was bought for preservation and ran on the Yaxham Park Railway in Norfolk. It is now at the Thursford Collection, also in Norfolk, and no longer steamed.

Wednesday 30th June 1965

Velinheli, another Hunslet 0-4-0 saddle tank, was also inside the Dinorwic Workshops that day. It was built in 1886 with the Works No. 409. Bought for preservation in 1965, it is now based on the Launceston Steam Railway but has been on the Ffestiniog and Welsh Highland Railways at times. A new boiler has been constructed for it at the Ffestiniog Railway's Boston Lodge. It is one of eleven of the lighter quarry locomotives with 7 x 10in. outside cylinders called the 'Alice' Class which were built by Hunslet for Dinorwic Quarries. All have been preserved.
Wednesday 30th June 1965

Penrhyn Quarries, Bethesda

There was quarrying at Penrhyn as early as the sixteenth century and it became the largest slate quarry in the world. Slate is still sourced from there but on a very diminished scale. The six mile long 1ft 10¾in. gauge Penrhyn Railway was opened in 1801, partly on the route of the earlier Llandegai Tramway. Its purpose was to transport slate from the quarries at Bethesda to Port Penrhyn near Bangor. It closed on 24th July 1962. There was an attempt to preserve and operate a short restored section of the line from Felin Fawr but this seems to have come to an end in 2017 after five years.

Stanhope, a Kerr, Stuart 'Tattoo' Type 0-4-0 saddle tank built in 1917 (Works No. 2395), in the withdrawn locomotive line at the Penrhyn Works. It had had been sold to Lord Penrhyn's slate quarries at Bethesda in 1934 by the Durham County Waterboard which had used it in the construction of the Burnhope Reservoir. It had earlier belonged to Holloway Brothers contractors, who had used it at a housing estate site in Rosyth and then on construction of the Swanley bypass. Despite looking more like 'no hope' than *Stanhope*, after nearly twenty years out of use rusting outside the Coed-y-parc workshops it was sold for preservation the year after this photograph was taken. At first it was moved to Bressingham, where parts were removed, then to the Lynton & Barnstaple Railway Association at Landkey and after that to the Kew Bridge Steam Museum. Next it went to the Old Kiln Light Railway in Surrey and, in 1999, to Alan Keef Ltd to complete the renovation for the Moseley Railway Trust railway at Apedale near Newcastle-under-Lyme. *Wednesday 30th June 1965*

This was the bitter-sweet sight that met visitors to the Coed-y-parc Penrhyn Works at Bethesda in Snowdonia. The sad line of withdrawn locomotives resting and rusting, apparently beyond saving, in a sort of mini Barry scrapyard must have encouraged many a daydream and fortunately every one of them, except *Skinner,* has been preserved. Led by ***Eigiau, Stanhope***, the de Winton ***Kathleen, Jubilee 1897***, frames wheels and part of the cab of, I believe, ***Skinner, Lilla***, and ***Sgt Murphy*** await their fate with ***Lilian,*** which was next in line but out of sight. ***Eigiau*** is an Orenstein & Koppel 0-4-0 well tank built in 1912 (Works No. 5668) which was originally supplied to C.L. Warren contractors in Cheshire and named ***Sunlight.*** In 1916 it was sold to the Aluminium Corporation of Dolgarrog for use in building Cowlyd reservoir and renamed ***Eigiau*** after a lake in Snowdonia. It became a Penrhyn locomotive in 1928. It was taken out of service in 1949 and was bought for preservation by Mr G.J. Mullis and removed in pieces to Droitwich in January and February 1963 and restored to working order. It ran at Bressingham Gardens for some time but it is now part of the Bredgar & Wormshill Light Railway collection. *Sunday 10th June 1962*

The unusual de Winton 0-4-0 vertical boiler *Kathleen* in the line of withdrawn locomotives at the Coed-y-parc Penrhyn Works. It was built, not far away at Caernarfon, in 1877 with the Works No. 106 and was one of seven of the type used at the Penrhyn quarries. Another, *George Henry,* is preserved at the Narrow Gauge Railway Museum at Tywyn. *Kathleen* is now in the Vale of Rheidol collection awaiting public display. *Sunday 10th June 1962*

Named to commemorate Queen Victoria's Diamond Jubilee, *Jubilee 1897,* an outside cylinder 0-4-0 saddle tank built by Manning, Wardle in 1897 with the Works No. 1382, was rusting away at the Coed-y-parc Penrhyn Works that day. It had been taken out of service almost exactly seven years earlier, on 9th June 1955. It was built for the Cilgwyn Quarry at Nantlle but it was sold to Penrhyn Quarries in 1928. Fortunately, the year after this photograph was taken it was moved to the Narrow Gauge Railway Museum at Tywyn where it was cosmetically restored. In November 2016 it returned home on loan to the Penrhyn Quarry Railway as part of a project to create a heritage site but when that ran into difficulties the following year it found a new home in Aberystwyth at the Vale of Rheidol Railway. *Sunday 10th June 1962*

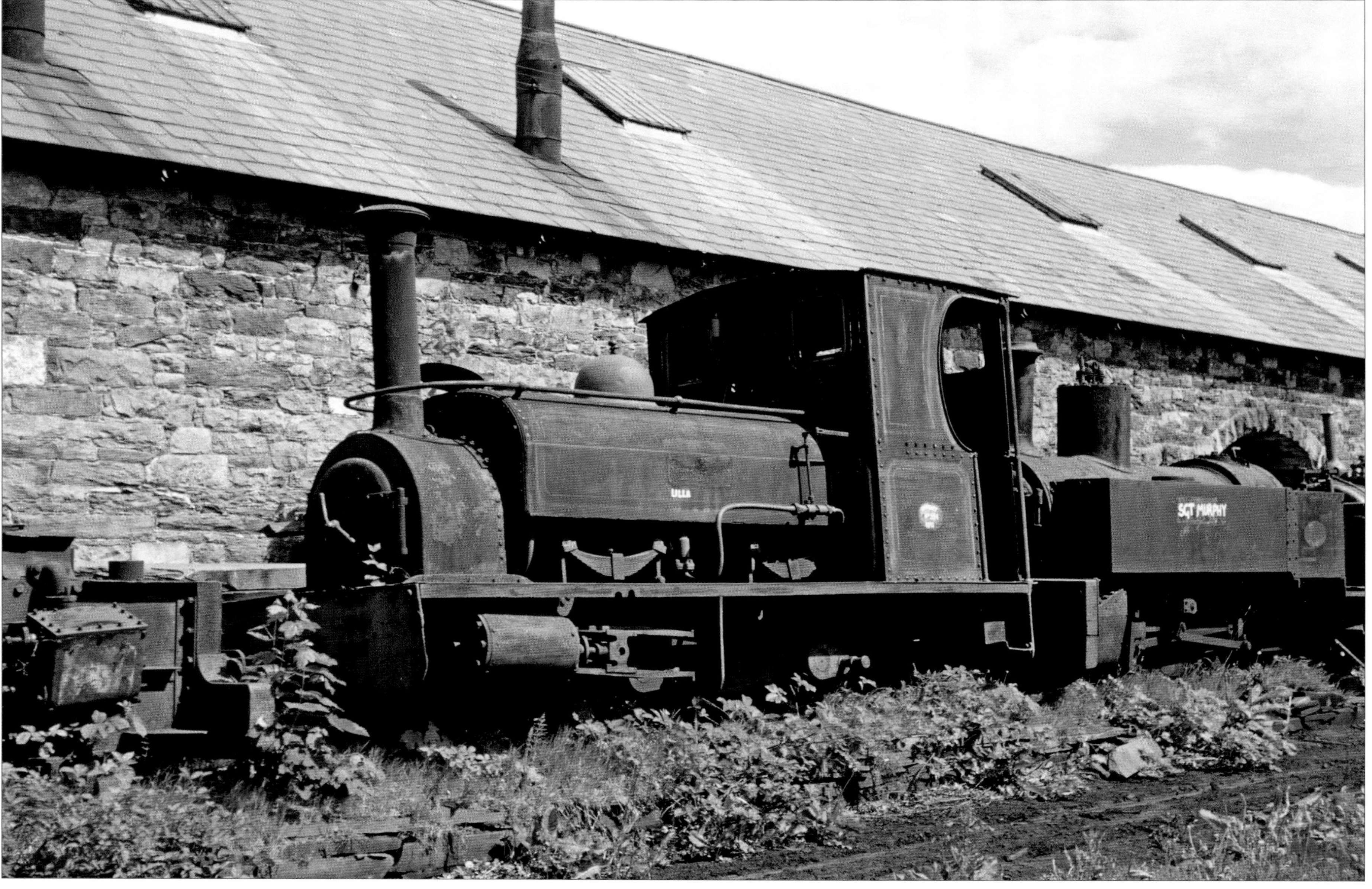

Lilla was also in the withdrawn locomotive line at the Penrhyn Works. It is an outside cylinder 0-4-0 saddle tank built by the Hunslet Engine Co. in 1891 with the Works No. 554 and delivered to the Cilgwyn Slate Co. Quarry at Nantlle. It was bought for use at the Penrhyn Quarry in 1928 and taken out of service with a failed boiler in 1955. It was acquired for preservation by Bernard Latham in 1963 and after restoration *Lilla* went to the Knebworth Park & Winter Green Railway from 1972 until 1987 and then to the Kew Bridge Steam Museum. The next move, in 1991, was to the Bala Lake Railway for two years before finally going to the Ffestiniog Railway where it was bought by a group of members and has been used mainly for local events and on short visits as an exhibit to other sites and railways. *Sgt Murphy,* an 0-6-0 side tank built by Kerr, Stuart & Co. Ltd for the Admiralty in 1918 with the Works No. 3117, can be seen next in line. *Sunday 10th June 1962*

Lilian, an outside cylinder 0-4-0 saddle tank built by the Hunslet Engine Co. in 1883 with the Works No. 317, in the line of withdrawn engines next to ***Sgt Murphy*** at Coed-y-parc Penrhyn Works. This was seven years after it had been taken out of service with a condemned boiler. As with a number of the Penrhyn engines given the names of members of the quarry owner's family, ***Lilian*** was named after a daughter of Lord George Sholto Gordon Douglas-Pennant, the third Baron Penrhyn. Fortunately, in 1965, the locomotive was taken to a site in Surrey where it was restored to working order. In 1983 ***Lilian*** moved even further south to the Launceston Steam Railway in Cornwall. It now runs there with a tender. Two other Hunslet locomotives of the same type, named ***Gwynedd*** and ***Winifred***, worked at Penrhyn and both have been preserved. *Sunday 10th June 1962*

Nesta, a Hunslet Engine Co. outside cylinder 0-4-0 saddle tank built in 1899 with the Works No. 704, inside Coed-y-parc Penrhyn Works with several other locomotives that were destined to cross the Atlantic. It went to the Hacienda La Esperanza Sugar Mill Museum at Manati in Puerto Rico but it has now returned to Britain for preservation and, after a stay in the Vale of Rheidol works at Aberystwyth, has been on display on loan at the Llanuwchllyn Heritage Centre at the Bala Lake Railway. *Wednesday 30th June 1965*

Blanche inside the Coed-y-parc Penrhyn Works, the month before it last ran over the Penrhyn main line. It was then bought by the Ffestiniog Railway and arrived there in December 1963. The locomotive was built by the Hunslet Engine Co. as a $10^{1}/_{2}$ x 12 in. outside cylinder 0-4-0 saddle tank in 1893 with the Works No. 589 and was one of three of the type used on the 'main line' from the quarries to Port Penrhyn near Bangor. It was named after the wife of Edward Sholto Douglas-Pennant. ***Blanche*** and ***Linda*** have since been rebuilt as 2-4-0 saddle tanks with tenders and they are now on the Ffestiniog Railway. The third, ***Charles***, is preserved in the Penrhyn Castle Museum.
Sunday 10th June 1962

Cegin, an Andrew Barclay outside cylinder 0-4-0 well tank built in 1931 (Works No. 1991), also inside the Penrhyn Works. It was supplied new to the Durham County Water Board and used for the construction of the Burnhope Reservoir where it carried the name ***Red***. It was sold to Lord Penrhyn's slate quarries along with a number of other locomotives in 1936. The similar locomotive nearer the camera is ***Glyder*** which was was named ***Grey*** at Burnhope. Both were exported to the USA the month after the photograph was taken as two of six ex-Penrhyn locomotives bought by an American dealer and auctioned there. ***Cegin*** and ***Glyder*** went to Indiana for display at a planned museum but they went into store when this project was not realised. It seems that, like ***Nesta, Cegin*** went to the Hacienda La Esperanza Sugar Mill Museum at Manati in Puerto Rico. It was repatriated to England in 2016 and underwent restoration at the Statfold Barn Railway. ***Glyder***, also repatriated, was steamed for the first time since 1965 at the Beamish Museum in June 2019. *Wednesday 30th June 1965*

Marchlyn, an Avonside Engine Co. outside cylinder 0-4-0 side tank built in 1933 (Works No. 2067), was another locomotive inside the Penrhyn Works. Like ***Cegin*** it was originally supplied new to the Durham County Water Board and used for the construction of the Burnhope Reservoir, where it carried the name ***Wear***, and it was sold to Lord Penrhyn's slate quarries in 1936. It was exported to the USA in 1965 and went to the Lake Winnepesaukah Amusement Park at Rossville in Georgia. It has now been repatriated and is to be found at the Statfold Barn Railway. Sister locomotive ***Ogwen*** (Avonside Engine Works No. 2066 built in 1933), also now at Statfold Barn, can be seen nearer the camera.
Wednesday 30th June 1965

Blanche's sister, ***Linda***, at the Ffestiniog Boston Lodge Works being overhauled after a derailment the previous September. It was built by the Hunslet Engine Co. in 1893 with the Works No. 590 as an 0-4-0 saddle tank for work at Penrhyn slate quarries on the Port Penrhyn 'main line'. At this time it was on hire from Penrhyn Quarries but it was purchased at the end of 1963. As with a number of the Penrhyn engines, ***Linda*** was given the name of a member of the quarry owner's family. Linda Blanche Douglas-Pennant was the daughter of Edward Sholto Douglas-Pennant. *Saturday 13th July 1963*

Linda, still an 0-4-0 saddle tank locomotive but attached to the modified tender from the locomotive ***Welsh Pony***, had been bought from Penrhyn Quarries and was fully part of the Ffestiniog Railway fleet when seen here at Porthmadog (known by its English form 'Portmadoc' at the time). Its cab had been re-profiled to allow for clearance in Garnedd tunnel. In 1970 it was converted into a 2-4-0 saddle tank with tender. It, and ***Blanche***, ran for some years as oil-burners but both are now coal-fired again. *Sunday 10th April 1966*